JUST BE
THE BANK

JUST BE THE BANK

Rewire Your Brain to Win *The Money Game,*
Beat Wall Street and Make Double-Digit Returns
through **Private Lending**

DAVE STECH, JOSH STECH, AND BLAKE STECH

CERTIFIED

(H)

WRITTEN
BY HUMAN

Testimonials

"What I've learned at Just Be The Bank is allowing me to build a legacy for my children and become a passive-active investor. Dave's the man, he's been there and done it, and that gives me the confidence to take the next step in my real estate investing."

Bill Hyman,
Los Angeles,
CA Orthodontist

"Private lending has been a life changer and a game changer for my family. The training we received at Just Be The Bank has taken our business to the next level. Our experience has been invaluable."

Randy Cline,
Marshville,
North Carolina Retired Dentist,
Private Lender

"I wanted you, Dave, Josh, and Blake to know how much I personally appreciate you creating the Just Be the Bank workshop. I have dreamed of having a family business for years. My partner was always busy growing his insurance company, and I was busy with the kids and real estate. Now that the kids are grown and the businesses are established, we finally have the time to focus on creating a family business/legacy, and JBB is a perfect fit for us! Family is our highest priority, and it's clear that it's JBB's top priority as well."

Michele McTeague

"I LOVE what you've done with the Stech Family Office, Dave! I plan to follow your lead one day by accumulating wealth and creating my own Family Office to help my family stay connected in a productive way while consistently growing personally & professionally. I also love you & your family's mindset when it comes to time, health, and accumulating wealth by doing good, having fun, and making money! Thanks for the inspiration."

Dr. Naren C.

"There are certain people that have significantly impacted my life, from a philosophical or a financial perspective, and Dave you are one of them, and by extension your sons also. And that list of people for me is quite short. I will always be extremely grateful to you, and glad you consider me in your circle of friends. The time Josh and Blake put into this, as well as all the other things Josh does, is amazing, but hell they're young and can go 24/7. As Cooper said to me, wherever Dave goes, I'll be hanging on to his coat tails. I said I'll be right there next to you. Thanks!"

Dr. Robert U.

"Honestly, in the world we live in, it is hard to imagine people going so far out of the way to help other people get ahead. I sometimes am in disbelief that all of this is even real. Doesn't there have to be a catch somewhere? And when I get over my tendency to be suspicious, I fall back into a state of disbelief. Too good to be true!!! Thank you, Thank you, Thank you!"

Laura B.

"Mr. Dave, many times I've shared my appreciation with you for all of the time, effort, and resources that you and your family invest into Just Be The Bank. Specifically, this time, I want to thank you for opening so many doors into a world of investing that I never would have achieved access to without you, but also for the example you set as a father. I enjoy watching you and your 'boys' work together in JBB, and it challenges me to find more opportunities for my boys and me to work and have fun as well, especially as they get older. Thanks for the inspiration."

Dr. John H.

"Hi Dave :). I am SO appreciative of what YOU, Josh, and Blake are doing in MY life. The fact that none of you NEEDS to do this, but are WILLING to go to ALL the trouble, time, research, teaching, I am just in awe. The simple fact that you decided to take time out of your personal life(s) so you can HELP others and make others' lives better, bless lives for generations to come; there are no words to express my heartfelt, sincere "thank you." You and your sons will be blessed for doing this! I love being a part of this group and can't thank each of you enough. Can't wait to meet all of you in San Diego!!! Eternally grateful…"

Susan Zachary

"I know, you have heard this before… seriously, I can't thank you enough for what you've provided me with as I "rewire" from being a dentist to being an investor. The knowledge I have received thus far is incredible not to mention the opportunities of listening (trying to understand) some of the most intelligent individuals in their respective industries! It's like drinking from a firehose at times :). The education we have been afforded is mind-blowing, and the generosity the Stech Family has shown is beyond comprehension! Thank you!!"

Dr. Cary G.

"I can honestly say that your family – Kellen and Kathy included :) – has been a tremendous blessing not only to our family but to the entire Just Be The Bank community. Your level of intensity and preparation is unmatched. It is very evident that each member of the team works tirelessly to maximize and leverage each individual's respective talents and knowledge in order to create an amazing educational experience in combination with investing opportunities that we would otherwise never have access to. It is with much gratitude and appreciation that I write this ... THANK YOU!"

Dr. Aaron M.

Dedication

Gayle/Momma, you are the foundation of it all. You gave us your best so we could become our best. Your love, loyalty, and belief in us built the men we are and made this all possible. Without you, there is no us.

DISCLAIMER

The material contained in this book is for informational purposes only.

The authors are not certified financial planners or professional tax advisors. All stories shared are based on personal experience and should not in any way be construed as individualized financial advice.

While it is our family's hope that you will find our examples and experiences illuminating and inspirational, please do your own due diligence. As needed, seek out professional financial and tax advice from someone familiar with your unique financial situation, and follow the guidance of your own knowledgeable advisors if you choose to pursue private lending.

A Note to the Reader

This book is a collaboration between Dave Stech (yours truly) and my sons and business partners Josh Stech and Blake Stech. Each of us has had a hand in developing the ideas that you'll find in the book. To make it easy for you to follow as you read, we've written the book in my voice.

Here's to your success!

Dave Stech
Feb. 8, 2025
San Juan, Puerto Rico

CONTENTS

Introduction *1*

1. Make Money, Do Good, Have Fun 9
2. Recalibrating Your Money Lens 19
3. Winning at the Money Game 37
4. Ditch Wall Street—And Escape the Game You Were Never
   Meant to Win 53
5. Speed, Greed, and the Power of Private Lending 65
6. The 5 Deal Killers 79
7. Every Lender Needs a Credit Policy 97
8. The Tax-Free Way to Do Private Lending 119
9. From One Deal to a Dynasty: Launching Your Private
   Lending Empire 135

Conclusion *149*
Bonus Chapter: From Red Shield to Rothschild—The Original Private
Lender Playbook *157*
About the Authors *167*

Introduction

"Money is like a sixth sense – and you can't make use of the other five without it."
- William Somerset Maugham

If I could help you add a zero to your income and net worth, how would your life look different?

What would all that extra money *do* for you and your family?

These are bold questions. I'll own that.

But I've asked them a thousand times—from conference stages, at my workshops, and in private rooms with high-net-worth investors. And every time, I see the same thing: people wake up.

That's what I want for you.

I want you fully awake and paying attention. Because what I'm about to share isn't some theory from a finance textbook. It's an opportunity, as real as the chair you're sitting on—a means to radically transform your financial present and lock in a future that most people will never even glimpse, much less experience.

So yes, this book is about making more money. That's a given. But more than that, it's about what it *takes* to make more money. The mindset. The discipline. The right few moves that separate the dreamers and the dabblers from those who actually turn ambition into empire.

And yet, even that isn't the whole picture.

Because it can't just be about the money.

At the end of the day, this is a book about *you*. Your family. It's about you doing something your ancestors may have wanted to, but couldn't: planting your family flag firmly in the ground and committing to build something bigger than yourself—a real, lasting legacy with teeth and staying power.

And it's about doing it all in a way that's sustainable, largely passive, and—dare I say—fun.

That's a big set of promises, I know.

But we don't play small around here.

Upgrade Your Family's Finances Forever

This isn't a get-rich-quick book. If that's what you're looking for, now would be a good time to cut your losses and chuck this in the garbage.

I actually resisted writing a book for years. I didn't want to be lumped in with the snake-oil crowd—the ones promising that if you just follow their "one weird trick," you'll be rich by 4 o'clock tomorrow.

I don't care about 4 o'clock tomorrow. And if you do, this book isn't for you.

This book isn't for the financial gamblers, either. If you're chasing the next crypto moonshot or penny-stock miracle, I suggest Vegas. **But if you want control over your financial future—if you've got a generational timeline in mind and you're out to build something that truly lasts—*being the bank* is exactly what you've been looking for.**

After all, making money in this lifetime is one thing. Keeping it? Growing it? Expanding it across multiple generations? That's where the real game is played.

These days, almost one in five American households has a net worth over $1 million. That's an achievement, sure, but it's not exceptional anymore.

You know what is? The families who hit that milestone, and don't stop. The ones who turn it into momentum. A snowball. Families who build values and systems that send their wealth into orbit, compounding year after year, generation after generation.

No shirtsleeves-to-shirtsleeves nonsense. No slow fade into irrelevance. Just a systematic, proven approach to money that ensures your family lives in comfort and abundance—not just for the next 10 years, but for the next 100.

You might not be there to see it. But you can be the one who sets it all in motion.

Freedom at Scale (Plus Protection from "The Big Loss")

A financially free future is useless if it comes wrapped in fine print.

That's what's always driven me crazy about traditional financial models and savings systems. They're designed to make you feel like you're in control, when in truth, you're just another cog in their machine. Fees. Restrictions. Caveats buried in 40-page prospectuses. You think you know what's happening with your money, but really, you're at the mercy of a system built by someone else.

Screw all that.

I believe in freedom at scale. Freedom without a governor or ceiling on it. The kind of freedom where I never find myself running into the walls of some invisible maze—no matter how big I want to go.

I'm talking about the kind of freedom Jocko Willink described in *Extreme Ownership*, where you "own everything in [your] world", and never let outside forces dictate how things go for you and your family.

In the Stech Family Office, our success isn't dependent on the stock market, the Fed, or the grifters in Washington. Bull markets or bear, cheap debt or not, we are going to win. Period. We control our deals. We know exactly why we're making a move. And we'll be the victor—not the victim—in any market.

That sets us free from the fear, uncertainty and limitations that keep most people trapped in mediocre returns—and frankly, mediocre lives.

And because we're not gambling on market cycles or making reckless bets, we've built a system that naturally protects against the world's volatility. Every deal is structured intelligently. We never, *ever* bet the house. We mitigate risk upfront, so even if a deal doesn't perform exactly as planned, we keep playing the game.

Here's what that really means: you could take everything we've earned to date away from us—wipe the slate clean—and we'd still come roaring back.

That's the kind of confidence I want you to have by the time you finish this book. **I want you to know, beyond a shadow of a doubt, that no matter what happens in the economy, no matter what Black Swan event shakes the world, you are in control.** That it's not about THE economy, it's about YOUR economy. And that you have the knowledge, the skillset, and the frameworks to turn the money faucet on whenever you darn well please.

That's real power.

And it's yours for the taking.

Why Stay Merely Comfortable—When You Can Achieve the Exceptional?

Look, you picked up this book. You've already taken a step most people never will. And you're about to unlock a strategy that gives you true financial sovereignty:

- **Passive returns** — so your money works harder than you do.
- **Active control** — so you never hand over the reins to Wall Street again.
- **Generational impact** — so your wealth and wisdom multiply beyond your lifetime.

And that's what I want for you, more than anything. Those three things. Actually, one more: I want you to have that lightbulb moment where you realize that not only is this 100% possible—even likely—for you, but that you're exactly the one to make it happen.

Of course, *realizing* it isn't enough. Knowledge alone won't change squat.

The goal is *action*.

Here's the thing: you're probably already successful. But no matter how far you've come, staying still—being comfortable—is the same as moving backward. If you're not actively thinking at a level above where you are today—if you're not deliberately pushing your financial position forward—you're leaving the door open for complacency to creep in.

And complacency kills generational wealth. Comfort is the silent thief. Comfortable is where dreams go to die.

So why settle for "comfortable" or "successful" when you can engineer something exceptional? Why stop at being just another high-earner or successful investor when you could build a financial machine that works for you, your children, and generations beyond?

And sure, maybe private lending won't be the strategy you ultimately choose. That's perfectly fine.

But I guarantee you this: by the time you finish this book, you'll see money differently. You'll have insights into a universe of investing that most people never even consider.

And if you're willing to take action, you'll understand why **private lending is one of the most accessible, scalable, and profitable ways to grow wealth**—without sacrificing your time or sanity.

So, let's get started.

Let's add a zero to your net worth.

CHAPTER 1

Make Money, Do Good, Have Fun

*"Doing well with money isn't necessarily about what you
know. It's about how you behave."*
- Morgan Housel

Let me start with the obvious: you didn't need *me* to get where you are in life. You got here, to this moment, without any help whatsoever from yours truly.

That's not to say your life's been perfect. You've faced challenges— some big, some small—but you've risen above them. You've done what most people won't, can't, or just plain don't. And for that, you deserve some serious credit.

You're already successful, in other words, like all the folks I work with.

But here's the thing. If you were the kind of person who could settle for "good enough," you wouldn't have picked up this book. You wouldn't be here, staring at these words, wondering what comes next.

You want *more*.

And here's the good news: *more is possible*.

I'm not just talking about your net worth, though this book could very well add a zero to it. I'm talking about something bigger.

Imagine this:

- You step off the hours-for-dollars treadmill for good.
- You replace long hours at work with meaningful time at home.
- You build a legacy of prosperity and well-being that your family can sustain for generations.

Sounds like a pipe dream, right?

It's not. And I'm living proof.

At the level I'm going to guide you toward, you can have it all. The financial freedom, the time freedom, the global freedom—the peace of mind that comes with knowing you're building something lasting and meaningful and good.

And getting there is simpler than you think.

The Question That Changes Everything

When I think about what truly drives success, one memory always comes to mind.

It's a conversation I had with my sons, Josh and Blake when they were little. Josh was five; Blake was seven. They were sitting at the kitchen table with me, wide-eyed, staring at me like I had all the answers.

I grabbed a napkin and one of their big Crayola markers. Then I drew a triangle with three circles at each point. I looked at them and said:

> "This is all you need to know to live a happy life. And when you master this, you'll have greater meaning."

These are the **3 things** that will make you and me **happy/happier**

When my two sons were 5 and 7 years old, I sat them down at the kitchen table and drew **TWO** triangles on a napkin.

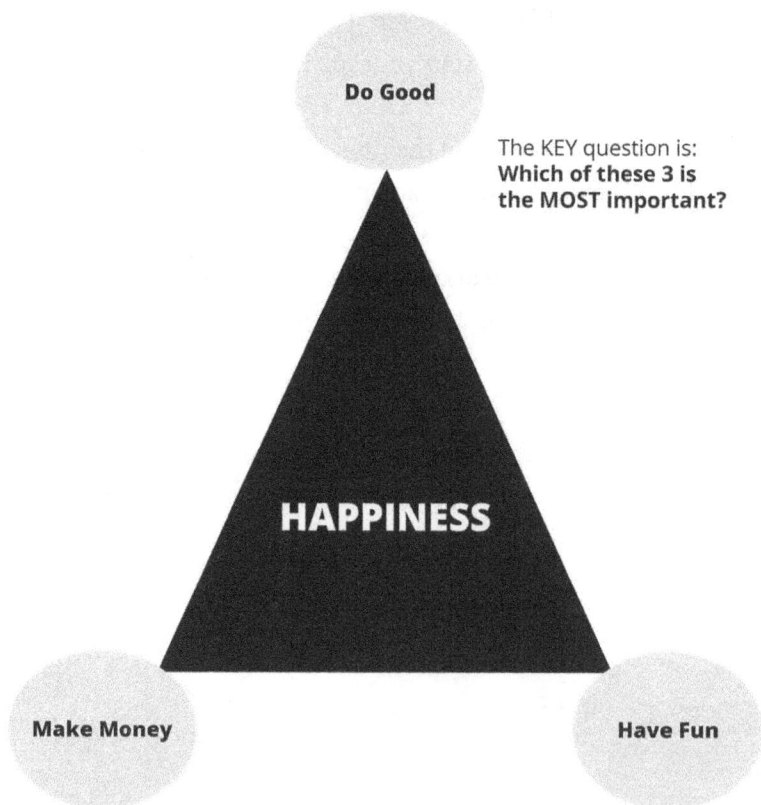

Do Good

The KEY question is:
Which of these 3 is the MOST important?

HAPPINESS

Make Money

Have Fun

The boys leaned in closer.

"See these circles? Each one represents something you need to be happy: **make money, do good, and have fun.**"

They stared at the triangle like it held the secret to the universe. And maybe it did.

"But here's the big question," I told them. "Which one of these is the most important?"

Let me ask you the same thing. And I'm dead serious now. Which of these three actions—making money, doing good, and having fun—is the most important for unlocking a happy, meaningful life?

Circle One Below		
Do good	**Have fun**	**Make money**

Grab a pen. Circle your answer. Don't overthink it—just go with your gut.

Done? Good.

Here's what most people say when I ask this from the stage or in my workshops:

- About 60% pick "doing good."
- Another 30–35% go with "having fun."
- A small minority—always less than 10%—choose "making money."

But here's the truth—and it's one most people don't want to hear.

The most important thing is making money.

Why Money Comes First

A lot of people choose "do good" or "have fun" because it's expected. It feels "safe."

As soon as you argue that making money is the most important, the mood shifts. People don't feel safe anymore. You can see it on their faces—suddenly, the room gets fidgety.

Why? Because somewhere in life, we were taught that focusing on money is greedy, shallow, even immoral.

But the reality is: money is the linchpin. The catalyst for everything else. Without money, you can't do much good. Without money, your fun is limited to what you can scrape together.

Let me make this real for you.

My family loves dogs. If you stranded me on a desert island and made me choose either a dog or a person as my companion, I'd choose the dog. Every. Single. Time.

I don't know if that's the case for the average Joe or Jane, but here's what I do know: when most people see one of those tear-jerker ASPCA commercials, they feel a pang of sadness—of compassion— and may even mute the TV or change the channel. In that moment, they truly feel for those animals. As they should.

But "feeling" is where it ends.

Why, though? If it hits them emotionally, why don't they *do* something?

One reason: they've bought into this idea that *feeling* compassion is enough. That it's a moral act on its own—an actual form of doing good. But it's not. It's a kind of spiritual participation trophy. These sorts of folks sit there, momentarily moved, convinced that feeling something from their couch is the same as doing something that actually matters. That empathy equals impact.

The second reason? Deep down they know: they don't have the money to make a meaningful difference.

We do. And we have. Over the years, we've fostered or rescued 14 dogs and donated more than our fair share to various animal shelters and causes. That's not just compassion—that's *cash-compassion*. And it's the difference between lip service and real contribution.

What about fun? The truth is, life gets exponentially more fun when you add a zero to your net worth. That trip of a lifetime? It's not just possible—it's an annual tradition. The Super Bowl tickets? Yours. The car you've been dreaming of since you were six? Parked in your driveway.

In our family, we made a simple rule: we take that trip of a lifetime every year. No budget, no guilt, no second-guessing. Just pure, unfiltered adventure.

For the last few years, that trip has taken us deep into the wilds of Alaska—to a remote fishing lodge perched on the edge of Iliamna Lake and the Kvichak River.

Now, this isn't some rickety campsite with a Coleman stove and a half-deflated air mattress. This is five-star wilderness.

The moment we land at the lodge, everything is handled. Food, guides, pilots, gear, everything. And no, it's not cheap—$30,000 for five days. But it's worth every dime.

There's no cell service, no distractions—just me, Josh, and Blake, standing waist-deep in the cold, rushing river, battling king salmon, sockeye, and northern pike the size of your leg.

And we can do this because of what private lending has afforded us. Because we've mastered The Money Game, we don't have to check price tags before making memories.

This? This is what winning looks like.

I'll leave you with something Balthazar Getty once said: "Life started getting good when I started making money."

If that makes you uncomfortable, good. Sit with it for a minute.

If you believe money is somehow bad or perverse, what happens when you start building big-time wealth? How do you reconcile those beliefs with your actions? And how do you think those beliefs will shape your financial outcomes?

The Lens That Shapes Your Life

This discomfort isn't about greed or morality—it's about perspective. It's what I call your "money lens," and it's probably the single most important factor in your financial life.

Your money lens shapes how you see wealth, risk, and opportunity. It influences how you earn, save, spend, and invest. And if your lens is clouded by outdated beliefs, it will hold you back—no matter how talented or hardworking you are.

That's why, before we go any further, you need to examine your current money lens.

Because once you know it's there and can see it for what it is, you can do something about it. You clean it, unwarp it—you can adjust it to blur out the B.S. and focus only on what truly matters.

And that's where the real journey begins.

CHAPTER 2

Recalibrating Your Money Lens

"Whatever your mind can conceive and believe,
it can achieve."
- Napoleon Hill

Your beliefs shape your reality.

I know, I know. You've heard it before. But let me make one thing clear—I'm not some tie-dyed guru peddling woo-woo promises.

I'm here to talk about money. *Your* money, and more of it. Specifically, how to make it work harder for you while you work less.

Less stress, more commas, I like to say.

But also more freedom and more control. More peace of mind, more zeros after the dollar sign. Sounds good, right?

Here's the kicker though: you'll never get there if you can't *see* yourself there.

Before we talk numbers, we need to talk about your *money lens*.

What's a money lens? Think of it as the filter through which you see every dollar, every deal, every decision.

It's not just about spreadsheets and bank accounts: it's the stories you tell yourself about money. The value you assign to it. The personality you give it. It's shaped by your lived experiences, the beliefs you've inherited, and yeah, maybe even a little baggage you've been dragging around without realizing it.

Most people—even reasonably successful ones—never stop to clean that lens. They hustle, they grind, they stack... but still, something feels off. No matter how hard they work, they're stuck just shy of escape velocity.

Why? Because their money lens is warped. Clouded. It's holding them back. And the worst part—they don't even know it.

When your lens is off, you end up sabotaging yourself. You trade time for money in ways you don't need to. You chase opportunities that drain you. Even when the world says you're doing well, it doesn't *feel* like enough.

Sound familiar? If so, good. That means you're asking the right questions.

Because if you weren't the kind of person who knew there was more, you wouldn't have made it this far. You wouldn't be here, right now, reading this.

The truth is, you're not wrong. There *is* more. And you? You could be more.

The question isn't whether it's possible. It's HOW.

I'll show you, but fair warning—this isn't going to be your typical rags-to-riches story. No violin strings, no neatly tied bows. To make my point, we're going to have to get a little messy.

Mayonnaise Sandwiches and Millionaire Dreams

Let's rewind to Indiana, circa 1960. To a trailer and mayonnaise sandwiches.

Mayonnaise sandwiches are the stuff of legend in my family. If you've never had one, they're not as bad as they sound—they're worse. Two limp slices of Wonder Bread slapped together with a dollop of mayo.

And yeah, they leave you hungry. But hunger has a way of teaching lessons. Lessons I didn't fully understand until much later.

My dad—Big Ern—was a man of iron. Literally and figuratively. As a 32nd degree mason and ironworker, he helped raise modern America, working on projects that brushed the sky: the Mackinac Bridge and the Sears Tower. He was one of those guys who didn't just build things, he embodied them.

Then came the fall.

It happened on one of the skyscraper jobs. Fifth story. He fell, and when he hit the ground, he didn't just break bones—the stability of our family shattered, too. For the next 22 months, Big Ern couldn't work. This old-school German who had *never not* worked a day in his life.

In that trailer park, there were no backup plans. No rainy-day funds. Not even any real savings. We survived on grit, resilience, and two of those godforsaken mayonnaise sandwiches a day…because we couldn't afford three.

But the root of the problem wasn't really the fall; it was Dad's *money lens*.

Big Ern was old school. No credit cards, no loans, not even a checking account. If it couldn't be paid for in cash, it didn't get bought.

In some ways, that was admirable. He avoided debt like the plague, believing it was the straightest path to ruin. We never, ever, lived beyond our means.

But there was another side to that lens. To Dad, money was something you *earned* through pain and sweat. The harder you worked, the more you deserved. Wealth wasn't something you could grow or invest—it was something you accumulated little by little, one paycheck at a time.

He never imagined that money could work *for* him. That it could be a tool, not just a reward.

Now, don't get me wrong. Big Ern was—and always will be—my hero. He fought on the front lines of a world on fire. Normandy. The Battle of the Bulge. The Kaufering IV concentration camp. He was there, parachuting into hell, liberating prisoners, doing things at 20 years old that would have most of us curled up in the fetal position.

Then he came home, picked up his tools, and helped build America. His hands built the skyline. His sacrifices shaped my world.

But those hands also taught me something else.

When you spend 22 months eating mayonnaise sandwiches in a trailer park, you learn two things pretty quickly:

1. Life is fragile.
2. Hunger can be a gift.

That hunger shaped me. It made me restless. Made me *think*. Because as much as I admired my dad, I knew there had to be another way.

And there were two things I wanted more than anything else:

- To be the kind of great dad Big Ern was.
- And to be a millionaire.

Not because I craved yachts or mansions, but because I wanted to make sure my kids would never have to know the taste of a mayonnaise sandwich.

So, I started searching. For answers. For opportunities. For a way to break the cycle without breaking my back.

And that's where the story really begins.

BTW, if you have a loved one that's nearing the end of their life, you should write them a letter now. If you'd like a guide, here's my letter to my dad: www.JustBeTheBank.com/dad I wrote similar letters to my mom and brother when they passed.

The Trap of the Traditional Path

Straight out of the gate, I had no unique, original plan to get rich.

I knew what I wanted—a million bucks to my name—but my money lens was pretty limited back then. It simply wasn't attuned to get my million bucks quickly or intelligently. I had no roadmap, no mentor whispering the secrets of wealth-building in my ear. All I had was my ambition and the belief that effort—*grinding effort*—was the way forward.

And since I couldn't "see" any other way to get ahead, I did what seemed logical: I took the traditional path.

First, I got an education. It was a big deal in my family: I was the first to earn a college degree. My parents, both of whom had stopped at the 8th grade, were beyond proud. Back then, a degree was still a golden ticket, a passport to a better life.

And for a while, it seemed to work. I landed a corporate job at Kodak, the 15th most profitable company at the time, and one of the biggest, most respected brands in the world. Up there with Disney, Coca-Cola, and McDonald's.

I worked hard. Really hard. Because that's what my money lens told me I had to do. And the harder I worked, the further I climbed. I earned promotion after promotion, grinding my way up the ladder until I became the youngest Vice President in Kodak's history—or so they told me. How do you really ever know?

Anyway, by my parents' standards, I was successful beyond their wildest dreams. My dad beamed with pride every time he told someone about his son, the corporate VP.

But here's the truth: I still didn't have my million.

And I still didn't have a plan to get there, either—at least not a good one. What I had was a handwritten table on graph paper—well before there were spreadsheets—thoughtfully placed in my 3-ringed daytimer that I carried everywhere. I updated it every month. Gray pencil for actuals and red pencil for estimates.

I had it all "mapped" out, if you can call it that. My single chart showed how I'd finally reach my million dollars at the ripe old age of 62.1. The whole plan boiled down to two simple steps:

1. Pay off my house as fast as possible.
2. Max out my retirement contributions every year.

Seriously, that was it. Those two steps. That was the full extent of my plan—because at the time, that was all my money lens could see.

So for 20+ years, I executed on it. Slowly. Dutifully. *Blindly.*

My "Lightbulb" Moment

It wasn't until the late 90s that I had my first real "a-ha." I remember checking my graph for what felt like the 5,000th time, and all of a sudden, the truth hit me like a freight train: my path to being a millionaire wasn't just slow—it was *too* slow.

"While I was busy talking about how much I wanted to be a millionaire, I was still thinking like a thousandaire."

For the first time in 20-odd years, I looked at my plan and saw it for what it was. Flawed.

If I wanted freedom *and* financial success—the kind that could sustain me and my family for generations—I needed something radically different.

So, I did what any slightly desperate, naturally hungry person would do: I took out a blank piece of paper and started asking better questions.

I'll ask you the same questions I asked myself:

1. What strategies are you currently using to make your first or next million?

2. Which, if any, do you feel are OPTIMAL? Like they're the absolute best way to get you to where you want to be financially?

3. And which, if any, of those strategies would you describe as working relatively fast, where the time your journey takes you to financial freedom is significantly compressed?

Do yourself a favor: pause here. Sit with these questions for a moment—really sit with them. Once you start to challenge the story your money lens has been feeding you, you begin to see cracks in the narrative. You begin to wonder, *What else don't I know?*

At the top of one of those daytimer pages, I wrote:

> **How can I win the money game and never have to work again?**

That one question lit a fire in me. I became obsessed—utterly, unrelentingly obsessed—with finding the answer.

Here's the thing I finally admitted to myself: while I was busy talking about how much I wanted to be a millionaire, I was still *thinking* like a thousandaire. I was playing small when I needed to think bigger. Way bigger.

So, I went to work. I filled notebook after notebook with plans, scribbles, and calculations. I tested ideas, scrapped them, and tested new ones. It was iteration after iteration after iteration until one day…

It clicked.

I figured it out.

And it worked.

In just a few short years, I transformed everything. I went from begrudgingly using the occasional consumer loan to becoming someone who made money work for me. I got smart about credit, leverage, and arbitrage. I stepped into entrepreneurship and turned my hard-saved first million into a far easier second million.

And then? It snowballed.

Fast forward a few more years and our family business was raising its first round of outside funding. Single millions became tens of millions. We'd figured out how to add zeros.

The transformation wasn't just financial—it was generational. My sons grew up watching and learning and doing, and together, we built something extraordinary.

But this story isn't about me.

It's not even about my family.

This story is about *you*.

Because the transformation I experienced—the shift in mindset, the evolution in strategy—it's something anyone can do. It's not reserved for the lucky, the brilliant, or the connected. It's repeatable for anyone willing to put in the effort to learn, to challenge their assumptions, and to execute.

And I'm going to show you how.

In the chapters ahead, I'll give you everything I've learned. The strategies, the frameworks, the mindset shifts—it's all here. But before we can go forward, we need to step back.

Why? Because no matter how good the plan, you can't build real wealth if your foundation is cracked. And as I learned the hard way, the first step to financial freedom isn't a bigger paycheck or a better investment.

It's rewiring the way you think about money.

So let's start there.

What's Your Money Lens—And How Is It Shaping You?

The idea that shifting your views changes your results (the concept I opened this chapter with) isn't just self-help fluff. It's rooted in centuries of study and observation about the human condition.

In *The Psychology of Money: Timeless Lessons on Wealth, Greed, and Happiness,* Morgan Housel puts it simply: **all differences in outcomes come down to differences in perspective.**

Consider the famous biblical phrase: "Money is the root of all evil." Now contrast it with George Bernard Shaw's quip: "The lack of money is the root of all evil." Two completely different perspectives— polar opposites on the same spectrum of belief.

So where do you land on that spectrum? Which one rings more true to you? What arguments do you hear yourself making to justify being somewhere in the middle (as you almost surely are)?

Whatever your answers, they're all reflections of your money lens. And like every other part of it, they've been shaped by how you were raised, what you've experienced—and, let's be honest, by how many mayonnaise sandwiches you grew up eating.

"All differences in outcomes come down to differences in perspective."

-Morgan Housel

I can look back now and be grateful for the burning desire to escape the trailer park—it fueled my ambition. I'm 100% convinced that if I hadn't started there, I wouldn't be here. But I also know that pieces of that upbringing still stick with me today. Some of them serve me well. Others, not so much.

So let's talk about *your* money lens.

Take a moment right now to reflect. I asked you earlier about your strategy for making your first or next million dollars and if it felt optimal to you. That question was a warm-up for this exercise.

Now it's time to go deeper.

Your money lens is the invisible set of beliefs that shapes how you relate to money. Where it comes from. What you're allowed to do with it. What it says about you if you have a lot—or very little.

These beliefs aren't always logical. They're inherited, absorbed, reinforced. And often, they're completely unconscious.

So let's bring them to the surface.

Think about how you were raised. What you heard your parents say. What you saw in your community. What you absorbed without even realizing it. Then, write down a few statements that reflect your deepest beliefs about money.

They might sound like:

- *Money doesn't grow on trees.*
- *If I just keep my head down and work hard, it'll all pay off eventually.*
- *Debt is dangerous and irresponsible.*
- *Money is meant to be spent.*
- *I should feel lucky and grateful for what I have—so why am I still stressed?*
- *The stock market is the best (or only) way to grow wealth.*
- *I'm not smart enough to be uber-rich.*
- *You have to spend money to make money.*
- *Wanting more makes me greedy.*
- *Rich people make their money off the backs of poor people.*
- *I'm the only one in my family who has to figure this out.*

Or, they could be more empowering:

- *Money gives me options.*
- *Wealth is a tool for impact.*

- *I don't trade time for money—I create value and get paid accordingly.*
- *Money flows to me when I move with clarity and purpose.*
- *I'm grateful, but not content.*

Now it's your turn.

Write down three to five of your own money lens statements. Don't edit or judge; just let them spill out. What do you *really* believe about money?

The clearer you get here, the easier it'll be to upgrade the beliefs that no longer serve you—and keep the ones that do.

Go ahead, put them down on paper using the space below:

_____

_____

_____

_____

_____

_____

_____

_____

Now read back through what you wrote. How's that lens looking?

If your reaction was, "Damn, my lens is pretty fuzzy," don't beat yourself up. It took me until my 50s to finally get a grip on mine. What matters is that you see it now. That you recognize your blind spots for what they are—and do something about them.

Change the Lens, Change the Game

Look, you deserve a life free from B.S. limitations—especially the ones you never consciously chose. That's what a narrow or outdated money lens does. It's one of those autopilot mental programs: it clicks on automatically, hums in the background, and quietly suffocates what you believe you're allowed to earn, build, or become.

Awareness is the first step toward change. And if you've made it this far, you're already waking up to the patterns, stories, and assumptions that have silently steered your financial decisions for as long as you've been making them. That alone puts you way ahead of the pack.

The next step is trickier. Now you have to actively challenge and *change* those beliefs—swapping out the ones that limit you for ones that serve you.

Because once you strip away the old programming, the question becomes: *What new beliefs will take its place?*

For me, letting go of those constraints didn't just shift my beliefs—it changed the way I saw everything. I stopped thinking of money as something you grind for. Something tied to effort, titles, or whatever scraps you can squeeze out of a savings account.

Instead, I started to see money for what it really is: a game.

We call it *The Money Game*.

At its core, it's surprisingly simple. To win the game, you need to do three things:

1. Generate cash.
2. Accumulate wealth.
3. Keep both.

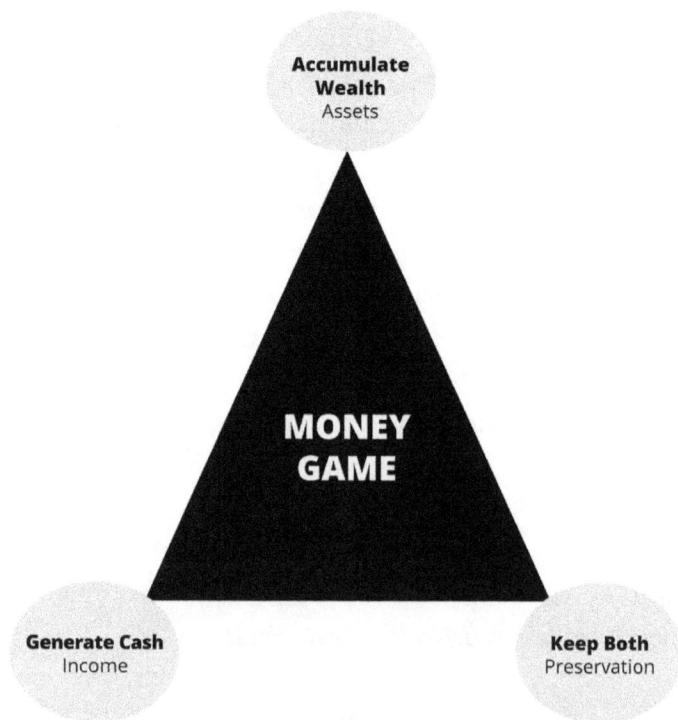

That's it. Three levers. Master them, and everything changes.

It might sound basic—but don't mistake simple for shallow. This framework transformed our family's trajectory. It's helped us add zeros to our net worth, build a family legacy we're proud of, and have a hell of a lot more fun than most people ever associate with something as dull-sounding as "money management."

It's also the foundation behind every venture we've built—including the multi-billion-dollar company my son Josh launched in his 20s using these exact same principles.

Now, zoom out for a second. Think about *your* life.

What might change if you stopped seeing money as something you *earn*...and started treating it as something you *play*?

What could become possible if you ditched your limiting beliefs, expanded your money lens, and finally started playing the game to win?

Take a moment to give that the thought it deserves.

And when you're ready, turn the page. Because from here on out, we're breaking down The Money Game piece by piece—and showing you exactly how to win it on your terms.

CHAPTER 3

Winning at the Money Game

*"To get rich, you have to be making money
while you're asleep."*
- David Bailey

Here's the thing about *The Money Game*: whether you know it or not, you're already playing it. Everyone is.

The question isn't *if* you're playing—it's *how well* you're playing. And more importantly, do you know the rules well enough to play the game to win?

Most people—including many ostensibly successful ones—are playing the game all wrong. It's not their fault. They're stuck running an outdated script, dictated by the limits of a money lens they don't even realize they have.

That's why so many people work so hard, achieve so much, and still feel like something's missing. They're trapped in a game they don't know how to win.

But here's the good news: you can break free of that script. You can play a better game. And I'm here to show you how.

The 3-Part Formula Most People Miss

The Money Game has just three strategies:

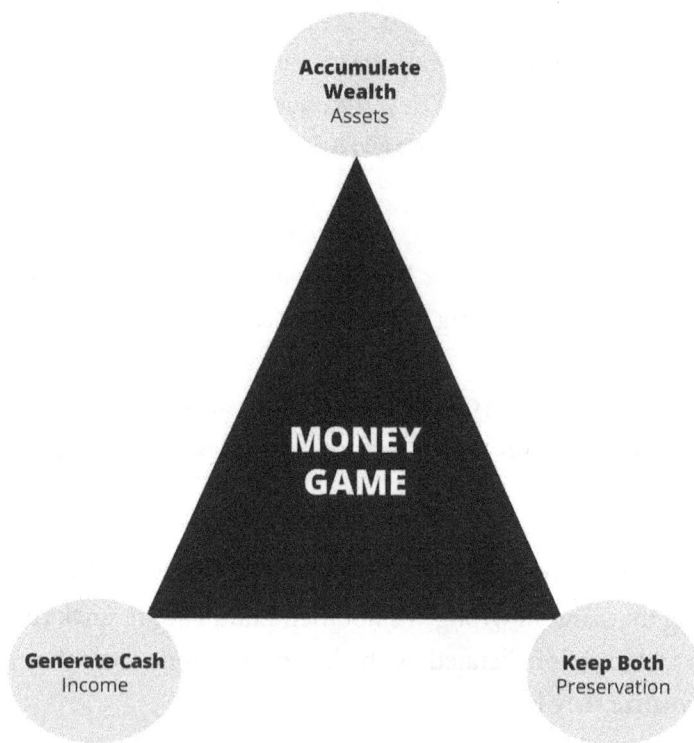

1. Generate cash.
2. Accumulate wealth.
3. Keep both.

Most people start with the first strategy: generating cash. They get a job or start a business to create an income stream. The catch? It's almost always *active* income. If they stop working, the money stops flowing. They're on the old time-for-money hamster wheel.

To mitigate this, they try to make more money—they get promotions, negotiate raises, grow their business. They're optimizing their hours-for-dollars equation, squeezing as much as they can from their time.

And kudos to them. I respect that. That's a heck of a lot better than just coasting.

The issue is, for most people, active income is where the game ends. They're playing one-third of *The Money Game* at best, and only solving for one of the three types of income (which we'll get to later).

The savvier folks start to move into the second strategy: accumulating wealth. They'll contribute to retirement accounts, buy a home, dabble in the stock market, and maybe even own the building where their business operates. They're acquiring *things* of value with their cash, aka assets.

"The question isn't if you're playing The Money Game—it's how well you're playing."

But even here, most people only scratch the surface. They don't fully grasp how to make their assets work for them—or how to choose the *right* assets in the first place.

And then there's strategy three: keeping both. This is where most people fail spectacularly.

"Keeping both" always takes me back to *The Big Short*.

There's this sequence in the film where Steve Carell's character (hedge fund manager Mark Baum) flies from Manhattan to Florida on a due diligence trip. He's after boots-on-the-ground intel, trying to answer two big, related questions: is the housing bubble real, and should his fund bet tens of millions on it bursting?

Baum ends up in a strip club, talking to a 20-something dancer during a lap dance. She's not shy about sharing her real estate portfolio. With a smug grin, she brags that she's juggling multiple adjustable-rate mortgages on each of her "five houses and a condo."

Five houses. And a condo.

The scene cuts abruptly, and the next thing you see is Baum back at the airport, on the phone, delivering the verdict: "There's a bubble."

In that one instant, he knew. The whole picture had crystallized right there in the strip club.

The stripper was crushing it in the "generate cash" and "accumulate wealth" departments, taking her nightly earnings and parlaying them into assets. But it was clear to Baum that she'd completely botched the "keep both" pillar of the game. Adjustable-rate loans on six properties? That wasn't just risky—it was like lighting a match next to a gasoline-soaked portfolio.

And Baum didn't just see one woman's blunder. He saw the systemic rot beneath the surface. A whole world of people generating income and buying assets but missing the most critical piece: protecting what they've built from risk, even disaster.

It's a perfect example of why "keeping both" isn't optional—it's everything. (By the way, keeping both is about more than just not losing it, as we'll get to later.)

The point is: **to truly win The Money Game, you have to protect your income and assets from all the forces conspiring against them.** You need to shield them from taxes, market volatility, shady money managers, even your own potential bad decisions. Most people don't do this well (or at all) and boy does it cost them.

Let me be clear—if you can generate some cash, accumulate some wealth, and keep most of it, you'll have a good life. A comfortable life. A life where you've got money in the bank and something to pass on to your kids.

But is that actually *winning* The Money Game?

Afraid not.

Why Even 'Successful' People Still Lose

Even people who *seem* to be winning The Money Game are usually playing it through a warped lens—limited, inherited, and full of blind spots.

Take income, for example. Most people only have one, maybe two income streams as part of their money lens: active income, and at best, a trickle of recurring. They understand clocking in, making a salary, maybe collecting some dividends. But the idea of writing a check today to get a bigger one back later—with zero additional effort—isn't even on their radar.

It's the same with wealth accumulation (aka assets). For most folks, the only store-of-value asset they'll ever own is one they would have bought anyway: their home. That's the original American Dream, after all.

And I get it. I was right there for most of my life. With my initial trailer-park money lens, paying off that mortgage and owning my home outright felt like the win of a lifetime. It gave me security. Pride. It was proof that I'd "made it."

But eventually I realized: a home doesn't equal a portfolio. Not even close. It's just one asset, bought largely for lifestyle reasons, that rarely "performs" in the investment sense. A kind of incidental asset, really.

And incidental assets simply aren't going to cut it. **If you want to win at wealth accumulation—and win big—you need *strategic, performing* assets.** Assets that generate income, appreciate over time, and allow you to use leverage to buy even more—with less of your own cash.

That last part is crucial. Leverage. Arguably the holy grail of wealth accumulation. For most people, it's just another word. Leverage only *becomes* the holy grail once when you reframe how you think about debt, and learn to see it for what it really is: a tool unlike any other.

My dad (heroic badass though he was) didn't get this. He only saw the dark side of debt; the side where you dig yourself into a hole using Other People's Money (OPM) to live beyond your means. He never had the ah-ha moment I did—the realization that money *borrowed* can actually lead to money *made*.

That's good debt. It's using OPM to "lever up" your capital and acquire more of the right kinds of assets faster, such that each one only requires a sliver of your own cash. That's not just smart. It's powerful.

My dad was right about bad debt, though. It's a sinkhole. A soft grave. Step even slightly over the line, and it'll bury you—draining your income, shrinking your options, and putting your financial freedom on indefinite hold.

And that's exactly where most people go sideways: they spend money on (or worse, finance) all the wrong kinds of assets. Swimming pools. RVs. Jet skis. Timeshares. Home theater setups. A new luxury car every three years. These things lose value the minute you buy them, and they're a cash *drain* rather than a cash *faucet*.

I'm not saying you shouldn't enjoy your life or have nice things. But those purchases shouldn't be your priority. Not if your goal is real wealth.

Real wealth comes from stacking assets with potential—cash flow, upside, or ideally both. Assets you control. Assets you can get into and out of at the right time, not just ride passively while crossing your fingers for appreciation.

Don't Just Own It—Leverage It: How I Bought a Home...and Made It Pay Me

Here's a real-life example to get your wheels turning.

My primary home is in San Juan, Puerto Rico—right on the ocean, with perfect weather and near-zero taxes. Life doesn't suck, as I like to say.

About a year ago, I bought another house in Fort Myers, Florida. I bought it for my wife—a place for her to nest, putz around planting things, decorate the way she likes, and make her own. A "home base" she can come back to if something ever happens to me, or if our backpack lifestyle becomes impractical down the road.

Now, I'll be honest: I bought that house near the peak of the market. Normally that's a huge no-no for me; I'm basically allergic to paying retail for anything, especially real estate when I don't see potential market upside. (That's one of my all-time favorite "accumulate wealth" strategies, after all).

But this wasn't an investment decision. It was a life decision. I wasn't obsessing over ROI; I was doing something for my wife. I was optimizing for the "have fun" and "do good" corners of the Happiness Triangle (see Chapter 1)—not stressing about the "make money" piece.

All that said, I'm also allergic to underperforming assets.

The thought of that house sitting idle, empty and bleeding money, while we're at home in Puerto Rico or traveling? That made me almost physically ill.

So I did what any cash-flow-conscious investor would do: I got creative. From day one, I structured it as an investment property. I partnered with a flipper friend I lend to—a guy who already runs short-term rentals in the area—and we listed it on Airbnb. He manages the bookings and handles the hosting, and gets a solid cut for his trouble. I sit back and watch the transfers roll into our investment account without lifting a finger.

In other words, I took a "lifestyle asset"—with no real appreciation potential—and turned it into a passive, positive cash-flow machine.

And if I wanted to take it further? I could lever it up. I could refinance the property, pull out 70% to 80% of the equity, and redeploy that capital into any other investment I want. High-yield private loans to flippers, for example.

That's the lens I live by. That's how I play The Money Game: **every asset needs to earn its keep. And if it's not going up in value, it damn well better be sending in checks.** Preferably both.

Which brings us back to the third pillar: *keeping* both your income and your wealth.

How the Wealthy Stay Wealthy

Uncle Sam is the biggest player in The Money Game—and he's not on your team. If you're not careful, he'll take a massive bite out of your potential.

Let me show you what I mean.

You may have heard this question before, but which would you rather have: a million dollars *today*, or a penny that doubles in value every day for 30 days?

If you chose the penny, good call. After 30 days, that penny would be worth $5.4 million.

Now let's add a twist you probably haven't heard: would you take that same doubling penny—but taxed daily at say 28%—or the million dollars upfront?

I'll spare you the math: you'd be way better off taking the million. That taxed penny ends up worth a pitiful $67,659.

DAY	EARNINGS	TAXED @ 28%	DAY	EARNINGS	TAXED @ 28%	DAY	EARNINGS	TAXED @ 28%
1	$0.01	$0.01	11	$10.24	$2.26	21	$10,485.76	$513.53
2	$0.02	$0.017	12	$20.48	$3.89	22	$20,971.52	$883.27
3	$0.04	$0.02	13	$40.96	$6.70	23	$41,943.04	$1,519.23
4	$0.08	$0.05	14	$81.92	$11.53	24	$83,886.08	$2,613.08
5	$0.16	$0.08	15	$163.84	$19.83	25	$167,772.16	$4,494.51
6	$0.32	$0.15	16	$327.68	$34.11	26	$335,544.32	$7,730.56
7	$0.64	$0.25	17	$655.36	$58.67	27	$671,088.64	$13,296.56
8	$1.28	$0.44	18	$1,310.72	$100.92	28	$1,342.177.28	$22,870.10
9	$2.56	$0.76	19	$2,621.44	$173.58	29	$2,684.354.56	$39,336.57
10	$5.12	$1.31	20	$5,242.88	$298.56	30	$5,368.709.12	$67,658.90

When I first ran the numbers, I thought I'd messed up somewhere. But I ran them again. And a third time. Same result.

That was arguably the biggest financial *ah-ha* of my life. I realized that taxation wouldn't just take half my money every year—it would eviscerate my compounding. Over time, it could erase 98.7% of my potential gains, just like it did to the penny.

In that moment, I saw it clearly: I had a silent partner in this game. A partner who never lifted a finger, but always took a cut.

The IRS. Aptly named, since, when you combine those letters, it spells THEIRS.

Now don't get me wrong—I'm all for paying my fair share. But I felt like I was paying *everyone else's* too.

And that was over just 30 days. Imagine 30 years.

That's Uncle Sam's compound impact. It's massive. It's vicious. And it's legally avoidable—if you know how to play the game.

But *keeping both* is about more than just taxes. It's also about *protection.*

Most people spend their entire lives focused on making money. But they spend almost no time protecting it. It's one of the biggest blind spots in the whole game.

Because wealth attracts attention. The more success you have, the more exposed you become. One bad tenant. One car accident.

One contractor who twists an ankle on your property. Suddenly, everything you've built is at the mercy of someone else's lawyer.

It's a harsh reality, but America is the most litigious country on Earth. If you don't think someone will come after what's yours, just wait until you have something worth taking.

That's why smart wealth players think in terms of structures, not just income streams. They don't leave assets lying around in their own name. They use entities to create layers between themselves and their assets. They make sure their insurance is dialed in. They separate risk from reward—keeping their operating businesses, their investment activity, and their personal holdings in different, discrete silos.

In short, they don't assume everything will always be smooth sailing. They play defense with as much intention as they play offense.

I'm not trying to scare you here—I'm trying to wake you up. Because it's not paranoia if it's true. And when you've spent years building wealth, there's no badge of honor for being "exposed."

The Stech Family Money Game

In my family, we don't just play *The Money Game*—we win it. We're constantly solving for it.

Here's how we do it:

- **We generate cash using more than just active work; we over-index on passive and recurring income streams (like private lending and cash-flowing real estate).**

- **We accumulate wealth using a broader range of strategic, performing assets.**
- **We keep what's ours by minimizing taxes, using intelligent structures, and mitigating risks.**

This approach allows us to "add a zero" to our net worth without falling into the usual traps:

- No trading hours for dollars.
- No limiting ourselves to "standard" asset types.
- No losing control of our capital or exposing it to unnecessary risks.
- No handing Uncle Sam more than he's legally entitled to.

And we do all of this through a framework I call *The 10-Point Blueprint to Win*.

Our family office's
10-Point Blueprint to WIN

If you add those all up, it's a **10-Point Blueprint** for **winning**
The Money Game (and not losing it).

My ONE question for you:
How many of those 10 are **YOU** optimizing?

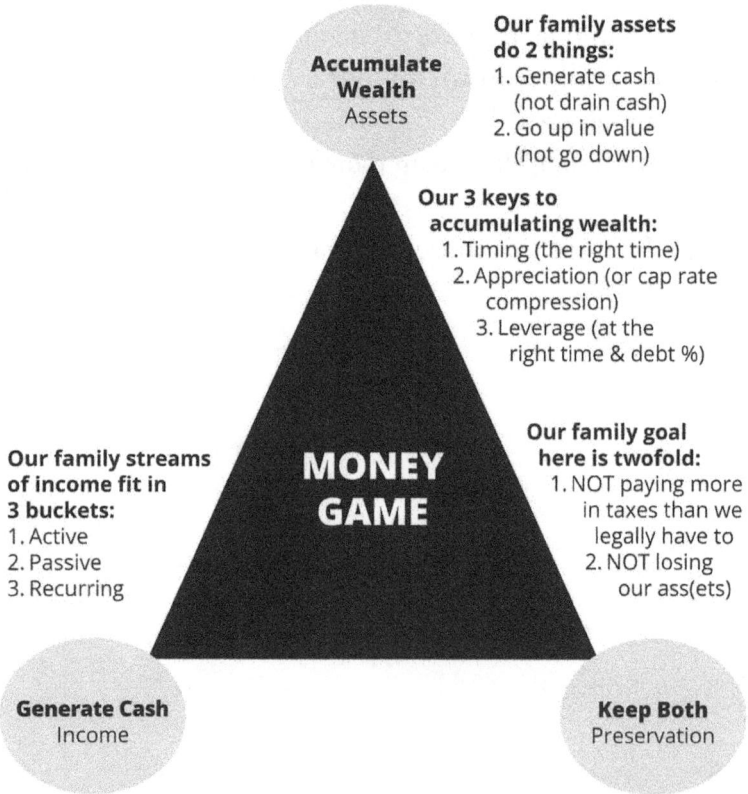

Accumulate Wealth
Assets

Our family assets do 2 things:
1. Generate cash (not drain cash)
2. Go up in value (not go down)

Our 3 keys to accumulating wealth:
1. Timing (the right time)
2. Appreciation (or cap rate compression)
3. Leverage (at the right time & debt %)

Our family streams of income fit in 3 buckets:
1. Active
2. Passive
3. Recurring

MONEY GAME

Our family goal here is twofold:
1. NOT paying more in taxes than we legally have to
2. NOT losing our ass(ets)

Generate Cash
Income

Keep Both
Preservation

Now, I won't walk you through every detail of the blueprint here. That's what the rest of the book is for. But I do want to highlight one key piece in the bottom right, a piece we'll be covering in depth in the coming pages: "not losing our ass(ets)".

That's not just a cute line. It's shorthand for a huge component of our blueprint. And it's the difference between winning The Money Game and bleeding out quietly while thinking you're doing everything right.

Because you can't grow what you can't keep. And most people don't keep nearly enough. Not because they're bad at making money, but because the system they've trusted is rigged, bloated, and designed to siphon off their gains before they even know what hit them.

So before we talk about what to do instead, we need to get brutally honest about what's broken.

That's next.

To learn more about our family blueprint, values, and lessons learned, visit www.justbethebank.com

CHAPTER 4

Ditch Wall Street—And Escape the Game You Were Never Meant to Win

"Three decisions that we all control each moment of our lives: what to focus on, what things mean, and what to do in spite of the challenges that may appear."
- Tony Robbins

A strange thing happens when you hit a certain level of success.

The moment you start making real money, suddenly everyone wants to help you manage it. Brokers, financial planners, wealth managers—they all come crawling out of the woodwork, each offering to take this "burden" off your hands.

It's bizarre, isn't it? You were smart enough to make the money in the first place, but once you've got it, everyone assumes you're totally clueless about what to do with it.

To be fair, they're not entirely wrong. Most of us aren't financial professionals in the certified, licensed, Wall-Street-approved sense. You've spent your time building a career or business, not poring over stock charts, decoding tax law, or geeking out on macroeconomic trends.

And honestly, why should you? You've got more important things to focus on. I certainly do. (Okay, I *do* geek out on macro trends—but that's my idea of a good time.)

But here's the problem: **when you hand over your wealth to these "experts," you're not just outsourcing the grunt work. You're offloading *control*,** and placing your financial future—your family's financial future—into a rigged yet unpredictable system. Into an incentive structure built to line *their* pockets, not yours.

Trust me, I've been there. I learned this lesson the hard way.

Getting Burned: My Six-Figure Loss Lesson

It was 2006. I'd left the corporate world behind, and I was 5 years into my journey as an entrepreneur (and loving it, by the way). The last remnant of my Kodak days was my retirement account—that same 401(k) I had diligently maxed out for 20+ years.

And shame on me: I was too focused on building my business to be intentional about what to do with it.

Rather than exploring my options, I took the *lazy* route. I punted it. A well-meaning friend introduced me to his broker at Merrill Lynch, and I handed over my entire mid-six-figure account without much thought.

Now, let me set the stage: my money lens was still fairly early in its evolution. I was taking some risks, but I was still pretty cautious overall. I told the broker I wanted my money in the *safest* investments possible. No risk. No experiments. Just steady preservation.

You already know where this is going, don't you?

By 2007, my brokerage statements were bleeding $250,000 in red ink. That broker made me *broker* all right. He turned my 401(k) into a 201(k), and I'm convinced that if I'd left it there, I'd now be eating Special K.

And my $250,000 was just a drop in a much larger bucket. Later that year, the CEO of Merrill Lynch, Stanley O'Neal, got hauled in front of Congress to "explain" their $8.4 *billion* in losses. You'd think this would be his moment of reckoning—a public flogging, a criminal trial, maybe even a stint in jail.

But this is Wall Street we're talking about.

Instead of throwing the book at O'Neal or shutting Merrill Lynch down, our so-called representatives in Congress bailed them out. Billions in taxpayer dollars poured into the same institution that had burned through retirement funds like they were Monopoly money.

And the cherry on top of this crap sundae—the part that chaps my ass raw: O'Neal walked away with a *$161.5 million* severance package, paid for by many of the same taxpayers whose money he torched.

A $161.5 million golden parachute, after losing $8.4 billion. Let that sink in.

That experience was a gut punch. It changed my life. It wasn't just the money I lost—which of course stung something fierce—it was the realization that I'd given up control of my financial future to people who simply didn't care. Meanwhile, they *make* money while *losing* my money. How's that for a racket?

As I tell my sons, other people and other businesses have wins and losses. Our family has wins and *lessons*.

So what was my lesson? I lost money because I got lazy. I outsourced responsibility and called it "delegation."

But here's the truth: **when you hand your money to someone who doesn't know or doesn't care—and it vanishes—you don't get to play the victim.** You made that choice. And if you made it once, odds are you'll make it again... unless you own it.

I made a promise to myself: never again.

The Problem(s) With Outsourcing Your Wealth

Losing that $250K woke me up to the two fundamental problems with the Wall Street approach to investing:

1. **You can't influence the outcome.** Traditional asset classes—stocks, bonds, commodities, precious metals, oil and gas—they're completely out of your control. Your money is at the mercy of forces so far removed from your daily life and your knowledge, you might as well be betting on the weather.

2. **You're trusting brokers, advisors, and money managers who prioritize their cut over your outcome.** Their entire incentive structure revolves around funneling your money into the same asset classes we just talked about—those that are (a) the most hands-off for them to manage and (b) the most profitable for them, not you.

Let's break this down, starting with the first problem.

The First Problem

Sure, a big portfolio of stocks sounds sexy. It looks great on paper. But the reality is, you have *zero* control over what happens to it. You can't nudge Apple's stock price or convince Walmart to bump up its dividend a penny. You're powerless.

Elon Musk? He tweets, and markets move. Governments tweak policies, and markets move.

You? You're just along for the ride. White-knuckling it, hoping the market doesn't chew you up and spit you out like so many others before you.

And it's not just stocks. Bonds, commodities, precious metals, oil and gas—it's all the same. Entire sectors can rise or fall because of decisions made in a boardroom or on a political stage, far beyond your control.

Now ask yourself this: **is there *any* other area of your life where you'd willingly give up that much power?** Would you let a stranger decide your career? Choose your spouse? Decide when and if you'll have kids? Choose your home? Plan your future?

Unless you're a high-stakes roulette player, I'm guessing the answer is no.

So why on earth would you do it with your hard-earned money?

The Second Problem

As far as I can tell, Wall Street operates under one core belief: *your money is better off in their hands than it is in yours.*

And they don't just believe it—they're convinced of it. They're 100% certain that a Series 7 license makes them the end-all-be-all of investing and thus *entitled* to your wealth.

And if you don't agree? Well, they'll just assume you're too stupid to know what's best for you.

But funnily enough, they have zero interest in curing your "stupidity." They don't actually want you to understand how any of it works.

Transparency on their part is just plain bad for business. The less you know, the more valuable they seem. Their whole model hinges on making investing a black box—so complex, so inscrutable, that you'd never dream of asking questions, let alone attempt to do it on your own.

"Wall Street operates under one core belief:
Your money is better off in their hands than it is in yours."

The more mysterious the system appears, the more Wall Street looks like a savior instead of what it really is: a smoke-and-mirrors sham.

Here's a fun thought experiment: if a market correction was on the horizon—and your broker knew it—do you think he'd tell you?

Highly doubtful.

Because wealth managers and brokers don't make their money by making *you* money; they make their money from commissions on trades, fees on assets under management (AUM), and, fundamentally, activity.

If your portfolio grows? Great. If it shrinks? They still get paid. Even if they wipe out your whole account, it's no skin off their back; they've already siphoned off their cut, trade by trade, fee after fee.

And if they *do* manage to make you a profit, those fees can wipe out a huge chunk of your earnings. A simple 2% annual fee might not sound like much—until you realize the massive toll it takes on your compounding over time…leaving you with only a fraction of what you'd have otherwise.

The High Cost of Fees

Comparing **$10,000** invested in the S&P 500 over the last 40 years to the same investment that incurred a **2%** annual fee.

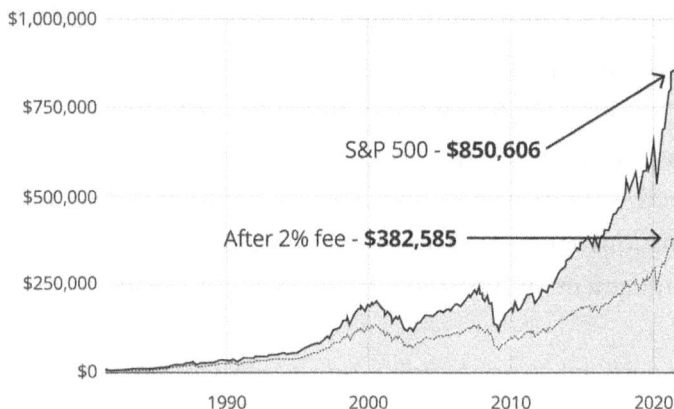

Just a **2%** fee eroded **55%** of the investment.

The point is, the pimps on Wall Street are quite literally paid to stay bullish. They need your money in the market or they won't make their precious fees. As long as they're moving your capital around, they're getting their cut.

So why would they ever tell you to pull back, when their entire incentive structure depends on keeping your money in play?

Here's the final irony: all that "activity" almost always underperforms the market itself. The brokers and managers who think they can beat the market by shuffling your money around fail 95% of the time. Just take a look at the chart below—over the long term, 95% of actively managed funds perform worse than just chucking your money in an S&P Index Fund and letting it sit.

Report 1: Percentage of U.S. Equity Funds Outperformed by Benchmarks

FUND CATEGORY	COMPARISON INDEX	1-YEAR (%)	3-YEAR(%)	5-YEAR (%)	10-YEAR (%)	15-YEAR (%)
All Domestic Funds	S&P Composite 1500	57.98	82.12	80.13	85.93	83.76
All Large-Cap Funds	S&P 500	63.46	78.64	76.49	89.15	92.43
All Mid-Cap Funds	S&P MidCap 400	54.18	83.28	81.74	92.68	95.13
All Small-Cap Funds	S&P SmallCap 600	72.88	93.59	92.90	93.36	97.70

And yet, they'll still smile, shake your hand, and collect their fees—whether they win or lose. Because in their game, the house always wins. The only way to break free? Stop playing by their rules.

It's Time to Ditch Wall Street—and Play to Win

Look, everything about the Wall Street machine is designed to enrich itself, not you. The commissions, the fees, the black-box nature of it—it all prioritizes their bottom line over yours.

So ask yourself: why would you trust a system that profits off your ignorance? Why would you leave your financial future in the hands of people who benefit more from keeping you in the dark than helping you succeed?

The truth is, no one will ever care about your money—your legacy—more than you do. And until you take control, you're just another pawn in their game.

This is why control is everything when it comes to winning The Money Game. And why the "Keep Both" pillar isn't just some throwaway bullet. It's a lifestyle. A worldview. A reshaping of your money lens where you bring your wealth in-house, keep it under your direct oversight, and take full ownership of the outcomes.

But let's zoom back out for a second.

Earlier, I introduced you to our 10-Point Blueprint for winning The Money Game. We've now covered quite a bit on the "accumulate wealth" and "keep both" pillars. You've seen how crucial it is to stack assets—the *right* assets—and how to stop bleeding it to taxes, fees, and lawsuits.

So let's finish the puzzle.

See, the whole blueprint runs better when you've got the right "generate income" strategy working in the background. And by "right", I mean a strategy that over-indexes on passive and recurring income (NOT active income), and opens the door to real financial freedom.

For us, that strategy is private lending. It's one of the most powerful tools we've found for winning *The Money Game*. Here's why:

1. **It generates near-passive, recurring income.**
    I say "near-passive" because nothing's truly set-it-and-forget-it. Every strategy takes some activity to start. But once it's running, private lending frees you from the hours-for-dollars grind. You deploy capital. You collect checks. And because you're lending on paper—not dealing with broken A/C units or busted water heaters—you skip the three T's: tenants, toilets, and trash.

2. **It helps you accumulate wealth.**
   Private loans command double-digit interest rates. Full stop. That means your capital grows faster, with less drama and more predictability than just about anything else out there. And over time, the loan portfolio you build doesn't just produce income—it *becomes* an asset. One you can sell, refinance, or pass down. (Granted, the way we do it, private lending is short-term in nature—but that's part of the advantage.)

3. **It protects your wealth from Uncle Sam.**
   This is the part most people miss. Private lending can be structured to grow *tax-free*. That's not hype—it's strategy. We'll go deep on this in Chapter 8, but know this now: compounding without taxation is a superpower. And it's 100% legal when you play by the right rules.

Take Back Control—Here's How

The rest of this book is dedicated to helping you win *The Money Game*—not just over the next 30 days, but for the rest of your life and beyond.

And if it's *your* life we're talking about, then it's also *your* money. Not Wall Street's. Not some faceless fund manager's. Yours.

So why not treat it that way? Why not choose a strategy where you're the one calling the shots—stewarding your wealth your way, in your own best interest, toward the kind of future you actually want?

"Private lending transforms the way you play The Money Game."

Private lending is that strategy. It ticks all the right boxes. It's smart, scalable, and simple enough to grasp, but powerful enough to transform your future. It gives you control, minimizes risk, and unlocks opportunities that most people don't even know exist.

And here's the good news: you're about to learn how to turn this strategy into real results.

In the chapters ahead, I'll walk you through the specific behaviors and tactics that set successful private lenders apart. I'll give you the core frameworks I've refined over 15 years of doing exactly what I'm about to lay out: the nuts and bolts of deals, the rules to live by, and the systems to protect and grow your wealth—while keeping *you* in full control.

This isn't just theory. It's a proven way to win *The Money Game*.

Ready? I hope so. Because winning doesn't happen from the sidelines. It happens when you step up, take action, and make the game work for you.

And taking action starts right now.

Let's do this.

CHAPTER 5

Speed, Greed, and the Power of Private Lending

"Money is multiplied in practical value depending on the
number of W's you control in your life: what you do, when
you do it, where you do it, and with whom you do it."
- Tim Ferriss

Imagine you're out running errands, and you bump into an old acquaintance. Let's call him Dan.

You and Dan catch up a bit, trading the usual updates about life, work, and family. Then, almost offhandedly, he mentions something interesting: "Yeah, so, I came across this house down the street from me—the place needs work, and the owner's in a hurry to sell, so he's willing to accept a low offer. I was thinking about buying and flipping it, but, you know, I don't have the cash lying around to pull it off."

"It's a heck of a deal, too," Dan says. "The guy only wants $200,000, and after about $60,000 in renovations, I could probably sell it for around $400,000." He shakes his head, almost laughing at the lost opportunity. "If only I had the money. Oh well."

You pause. "So you're saying you've got a deal where someone is basically handing you a six-figure profit, and the only thing stopping you is the cash?"

Dan nods. "Yeah. But, you know, banks don't move fast on stuff like this. And I don't exactly have two hundred grand sitting around."

This is where your money lens—your way of seeing opportunities—sets you apart.

"Well, what if I loaned you the money?" you say. "I could fund, say, 85% of the $200,000 to buy it and all of the $60,000 to renovate it. When you resell for $400,000, you make your profit, and you pay me back what I loaned you with interest. Win-win."

Dan blinks. "Wait, you'd do that? Just…loan me the money?"

"Not for free," you laugh. "But yeah, that's one of the ways I invest. I'm a private lender. And if I didn't have any money, I could 'broker' the loan to someone else who has the money, and I'd share in what they make."

Of course, it's not quite that casual in real life. There's due diligence. Legal agreements. A structured loan with clear terms. And Dan may or may not be the kind of guy you want to lend to.

But that's the core concept. That's the essence of private lending.

Why Private Lending Exists (And Why Banks Won't Touch It)

In our story above, Dan touched on something important: *"Banks don't move fast on stuff like this."*

They're slow as hell, actually. Glacial. Their whole underwriting process is "by committee," and they're so bogged down in red tape and regulation that they can easily take weeks or months to approve a loan—if they approve it at all.

But here's what Dan didn't say, and what most people don't realize: even if banks *could* move fast, they still wouldn't touch his deal.

Why not?

Because it doesn't fit their playbook. Their "buy box."

Think for a second about how banks make their money. A typical mortgage—it's a 30-year loan. That's not random. It's a business model.

Banks are all about *long-term* loans. They're in the business of collecting steady, predictable payments over decades. Their money isn't made upfront; it's made over time, through servicing fees, net interest margins, and compounding interest over years and years of payments.

Simply put: a loan that disappears in months doesn't feed the machine. So banks avoid these deals entirely.

Private lending works because it does the exact opposite of what banks do. It's short-term in nature (usually no more than 12 months) and built on speed—quick decisions, fast funding, and flexibility that traditional lenders can't match.

I call this Speed and Greed: the idea that if we can provide fast, reliable capital when and where it's needed, and we can reloan the same money more than once in a year, we can get the kind of double-digit returns that no commercial bank ever could.

Bottom line: **we're filling a gap in the marketplace that banks won't touch. And for that, we get handsomely rewarded.**

Even better, we get handsomely rewarded *no matter what the market's doing.*

This Strategy Works in Any Market Cycle

The beauty of private lending is that it's an evergreen strategy. It works in any market, whether it's booming, crashing, or just grinding sideways. Private lending isn't about timing the market. It's about controlling the deal.

When real estate is on fire—prices rising, bidding wars, low Days on Market (DOM)—it's because demand for homes outstrips supply. Deals move fast, and the people putting them together need to move even faster.

That's where a stand-out private lender thrives.

A flipper doesn't have weeks to wait on an "I'll get around to it" lender. He needs capital now. If you can filter and vet deals quickly, give them a fast yes or no, then jump into action if it's a "yes," you become as good as gold to that borrower.

Even when the market isn't red-hot, the need for capital doesn't disappear. It just shifts. In a "flat" or "slow" market, there may be fewer bidding wars and a bit less urgency, but flippers still need money, and they need it from reliable lenders who can move fast.

What about in a "down" market? Doesn't real estate investing grind to a halt?

Nope. **Private lending (and flipping) tends to be surprisingly recession-proof.** Downturns mean distress, and distress means opportunity.

Think about it: during economic contractions, more people lose jobs. More households experience income instability. Divorce rates tick up. Foreclosures increase. Life events force sales, and those sales often happen at a discount.

I call it the "4 D's": death, divorce, disaster or downsizing. Life happens, and not always in a good way.

The point is, flippers and investors don't stop buying. The best ones lean in, often scooping up even fatter-margin deals they can turn into outsized profits.

"Private lending tends to be surprisingly recession-proof."

For private lenders, this dynamic can actually increase competition for your capital and strengthen your position when structuring deals. You can tighten your lending criteria, demand stronger terms, and even command higher rates—not out of greed, but because your capital is simply in higher demand.

Look, the best investors don't stop working when the market slows. They adapt. They tweak their strategies, negotiate better deals, and keep their machines running.

In other words, they pivot. And I know a little something about that.

The Ultimate Form of Leverage

You know, I used to think success meant arriving somewhere. You grind, you hustle, you take the risks, and then—boom—you make it.

But if I've learned anything, it's that real success, whether in life or investing, comes down to one thing. *Options*.

When you have multiple great options, you have leverage. When you only have one? Someone or something has leverage on you.

Case in point: back in 2009, my son Josh was finishing up grad school at Stanford. One day, he called me with what he thought was a major life decision.

"Dad," he said, "I've got two job offers. One in consulting, one in investment banking. I'm trying to decide between the two. Which one should I pick?"

A binary choice. This or that. A single option.

Now, if you've been paying attention, you probably already know how I feel about binary choices. They suck. They box you in. They force you into a narrow frame—what I call the "Or trap". Psychologist Daniel Kahneman calls it the spotlight effect: *what you see is all there is.*

I'm all about great *options*. As in, several.

So I handed Josh a third: "Josh, if you go corporate, at some point, you're going to work for an idiot." I pointed at myself. "Why not work for *this* idiot first?"

Josh laughed, then went quiet. A few seconds passed. "Sure, Pops" he said. "Let's do it. But I get to be CFO."

That was it. The whole conversation. Two days later Josh packed up his car, left Palo Alto in the rearview, and gunned it for Sin City.

At the time, I was flipping homes—some solo and some with a close friend. When Josh came onboard in 2009, Vegas felt like an oil boom. A modern-day gold rush. We were snapping up foreclosures at the courthouse steps for pennies on the peak-dollar, flipping them fast, and generally clearing five figures per. Sometimes in just a couple weeks.

If memory serves, we did seventy-three flips in our first fourteen months. It was an incredible blur of Home Depot trips, rehab walkthroughs, and deal closings—one of the best runs of my career up to that point, bar none.

Until, just like that, it was over.

The government slapped a moratorium on foreclosures overnight, choking off our main supply channel like a tourniquet. What had been a steady pipeline of underpriced, high-margin deals slowed to a trickle.

The few bread-and-butter homes that did hit the auction block were getting bid into oblivion—prices so inflated they weren't worth the headache. In the blink of an eye, our once-great acquisition model was kaput.

So, we pivoted. Hard. We zeroed in on the one type of auction property nobody wanted—high-end customs—and instead of flipping them, we held. We spun up two luxury vacation rentals before anyone had even heard of Airbnb. Within a few months, both were pulling six figures a year at 25% cap rates; the kind of cash flow that makes Wall Street hedge funds drool.

Voilà. We'd cracked the code. Found a model that felt untouchable.

Or so we thought.

Then came rug-pull number two.

Clark County hit us with a cease-and-desist letter. Turns out the Vegas hotels weren't fans of competition, especially from mom-and-pop operators like us offering a "home" alternative off the Strip. So they did what big money does: hired lobbyists, leaned on the county real estate council, and got a prohibition pushed through. In Vegas, renting out a single-family home for less than 30 days was now illegal—unless, of course, it was on the Strip.

You know, Las Vegas Boulevard. Where there are no homes. Just hotels.

Oh, and get this. The fine? $1,000 per day, per property, indefinitely. Yeah, you read that right. We scrambled to sell our first property in 29 days, and paid Clark County $29,000 straight from our net proceeds at closing.

Poof. Another uber-profitable business model, gone. Two major "losses" in a row. Or rather, one major lesson.

What was the lesson? That pivoting isn't just a fallback, it's our superpower. That if we stay nimble and believe—deep in our bones—that we'll always find a way to win, we always *will*.

So that's what we did. We stayed nimble. We pivoted—again. We sold that first property for a nice gain even after the $29,000 extortion, and kept the other as part of our Family Office portfolio. Then we dusted ourselves off, got back in the saddle, and went hunting for the next big thing.

The Room Where It Happened

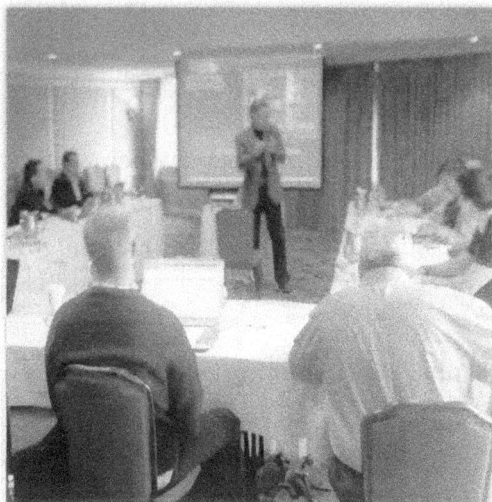

The exact day in 2011 that Dave (speaking) and Josh (bottom left, on his computer) realized how our family could win at the Money Game by becoming the bank.

It was 2011, and Josh and I were at a mastermind meeting in Tampa. A room full of sharp investors, operators, and problem-solvers. The kind of people who don't just kick around ideas, but actually execute on them.

When my hot seat came around, I laid it all out: our Vegas flips, the six-figure vacation rentals, the regulatory hammers, the forced exits. How we'd been crushing it, yet ended up 0 for 2 through no fault of our own. I held nothing back. My hope was to give people a badass case study they could model in more favorable markets, and maybe get some input from the group on our next move.

Then came the Q&A portion.

A guy named Mike, from Boston, raised his hand. "Dave, you just made a big chunk of change from that sale," he said. "How about you lend me some of it for a flip I'm doing?"

At the time, I could barely spell *private lending*. It wasn't on my radar. Wasn't something I'd ever even considered.

But it just kind of…clicked.

We had money. What if—instead of tying it up in another property, dealing with tenants, toilets, or a market that could turn against us—we loaned the money to someone else?

A new option. A better option, potentially. And you know how I love options.

So we funded the deal. Thirty-one days later, Mike closed the resale and wired our principal back, with interest.

The return? A massive 58.9% annualized. Not typical, but real. Hell, I've still got the wire receipt to prove it.

That was all it took. One deal, one near-60% yield, and I was hooked—in the best possible way.

That little experiment changed everything. We never looked back. Mike's single, oh-by-the-way deal lit a fuse that reshaped our future—and made private lending the engine behind our family's entire "add a zero" wealth strategy.

Fourteen years and 10,000+ loans. All set in motion by one game-changing shift.

And the best part? On our generational timeline, we're just getting started.

Private Lending Is a Skillset, Not Just an Investment

Most people treat investing like a transaction. As something they *do*. Buy a stock, purchase a rental property, toss money into a mutual fund, whatever.

But the reality is, **the best investments aren't just about where you park your money. They're about what you *know*.**

Investing isn't an activity, in other words. It's a skillset.

Skills are what separate someone who dabbles in investing and someone who consistently wins at *The Money Game*. Real, learnable skills. Evaluating deals. Vetting people. Structuring terms. Mitigating risk. Making moves with your eyes open.

And the best part? Once you build that muscle, you can flex it anywhere.

Think about this: when you lob money into an S&P 500 ETF, what brainpower did that really take? What life skills did you hone in that process?

None, I'd argue. I mean, sure—you made a decision. And if the market cooperates, you'll get a monetary return.

But nothing about that move made you a savvier human being. Nothing gave you an edge. There's nothing you could pass down to your kids to set *them* up to make better decisions—and preserve and grow what you've worked so hard to build.

And one thing I know for sure: **what you don't learn, your kids will inherit.** Blind spots included.

With private lending, yes, the returns are there. Double-digit, and more consistent than any other cash-flow vehicle we've found.

But the real win? You start *thinking* like a bank.

And when you think like a bank, you move differently in the world. Plain and simple.

- You see money for what it truly is: a Swiss army knife. Not a nest egg, not a life raft. A multi-pronged lever. One that generates predictable, repeatable, scalable returns.
- You get to stop gambling on market rallies and start architecting your outcomes. You're no longer hoping for tailwinds or appreciation. You're setting your own course.

Because hope is NOT a strategy.

Instead, you *engineer* your returns. You move your chess pieces around intentionally to play the game you want, and set up the future you envision.

That's why private lending isn't just another way to invest—it's an entirely new way to play *The Money Game*.

CHAPTER 6

The 5 Deal Killers

"Don't be afraid to give up the good to go for the great."
- John D. Rockefeller

Rule #1 of private lending: You make money by saying "no" to everything that isn't a great deal.

Simple, really.

But that raises the obvious question: how do you tell a great deal from a mediocre one—or a downright clown show?

Or worse: one that *looks* like a slam dunk, but isn't. The kind with hidden flaws that don't show up until you're deep in the deal. Miss them, and that slam dunk becomes a faceplant.

The good news is: these traps are 100% avoidable.

I cut my teeth flipping and developing in some of the wildest real estate markets in the country—Las Vegas during the foreclosure feeding frenzy, South Florida in the middle of post-Katrina chaos. I've seen deals unravel. I've watched investors take reckless bets. But more importantly, I've learned exactly how to sidestep the landmines, and how to help others do the same.

That's what this chapter is about: helping you spot the deal-killers before they blow up. The better you get at identifying red flags early, the smoother—and safer—your private lending journey will be.

Experience is the best teacher. But this book? It's your cheat code.

Let's dive in.

Deal Killer #1: Paying Too Much for the Property

The first deal killer is simple but deadly: the property has to be bought right. If your borrower overpays at acquisition, the deal is on shaky ground from day one.

So, what does "buying right" actually mean in the context of private lending?

Every property has an "as-is" value—what the market would pay for it today, untouched, before a single nail is hammered or coat of paint applied. If that number is $100,000 and your flipper locks the property down for $80,000 or $90,000, that's buying it right. They've created *instant* equity, built-in cushion, and given your loan a margin of safety.

But if they pay $110,000 or $120,000? That's buying it wrong. They're underwater before the demo crew even shows up. And if anything goes sideways—as they sometimes do—that initial mistake just keeps compounding.

Newbie flippers mess this up way too often. But it's not just a rookie mistake; even seasoned pros can get caught chasing deals—especially in hot markets, when emotions creep in and FOMO starts posing as a business strategy.

Lending In the Real World: Buying It Wrong

Let me tell you about a deal we passed on in Columbus, OH—a red-hot market as of this writing.

A guy named Nate brought us a flip opportunity: a little 3-bed ranch in a quiet, working-class neighborhood. Good bones. Nice curb appeal. He had it under contract for $155,000 and planned to put $28,000 into cosmetic upgrades: kitchen, paint, flooring, light landscaping. On paper, it sounded like a solid, bread-and-butter deal.

Of course, deals don't happen on paper.

We ran our own comps and quickly spotted a problem: the top resale in that neighborhood—same square footage, same layout, similar upgrades to what the borrower was planning—had sold for $185,000 just two weeks earlier. And it had a garage. Nate's didn't.

That meant there was no margin. No spread. Best case, Nate would break even. Worst case, he'd lose money, fall behind on payments, and trigger exactly the kind of principal risk we work hard to avoid.

He'd made a classic newbie blunder: he took the seller's number at face value. He price-anchored to what the seller *wanted* for the house, not what the market would actually support.

He hadn't bought it right, in short. And he didn't have a clear path to profitability as a result.

So we passed. We stayed true to our playbook, found a quick reason to say no, and moved on.

What's the lesson? **As the lender, you don't just fund the deal— you inherit the borrower's blind spots.** Always do your own homework. Always verify the value. Because if the numbers don't work at acquisition, they're not going to magically work later.

Deal Killer #2: The Rehab Goes Over Budget

One of the biggest levers in the flip equation is the rehab budget. Bar none. It's the domino that sets everything else in motion—not just the home's final look and buyer appeal, but also the timeline, the risk profile, and ultimately, the flipper's profit (or lack thereof).

To get a handle on it, you need a scope of work (SOW). A deal's not even worth reviewing without one. Only a third-rate borrower would pitch a flip without a SOW. This doc lays out every renovation item needed to hit the target resale value—and gives you a clear roadmap for how the borrower plans to get there.

But here's the reality: real estate rehabs are rarely smooth. The moment walls come down or floors come up, unexpected costs can start piling up like unpaid bar tabs.

That's why a contingency buffer isn't a nice-to-have. It's essential. Smart borrowers build in breathing room from the start. If they don't—if the numbers are tight and there's no cushion—it's a definite red flag. One wrong turn on a razor-thin budget can turn a decent deal into a full-blown quagmire.

What Happens When Rehabs Go Over Budget

If the rehab costs start ballooning mid-project, two things happen— neither of them good.

- First, the timeline stretches. That means higher holding costs for the borrower, more stress for everyone, and a greater chance of a market shift working against you.

- Second, the flipper's profit margin shrinks—or vanishes completely. And when that happens, your borrower may struggle to repay you on time. Worst case? You're forced to foreclose and take the property back.

Now for the good news: if the deal is structured correctly, rehab costs shouldn't hurt you. In fact, they can (and should) work in your favor.

Let's say the flipper has a solid plan. They buy the house below market value, creating an instant equity cushion in the deal. They then execute a *targeted* $30,000 rehab—"targeted" because the improvements are purely need-to-have. The kind of upgrades that cost $1 but look like $2 to the buyer—intentional, high-impact changes that add $60,000 in resale value on that $30,000 budget.

That's called *forced appreciation*. And it's how savvy investors turn beat-up properties into five- or six-figure paydays.

But here's the catch: forced appreciation only works if the rehab is dialed in—planned well, managed tightly, and kept on budget. Otherwise, that $30,000 rehab creeps to $50,000...then $75,000... while the added value is still $60,000. Now the flipper's upside down and struggling to cover cost overruns.

And your monthly interest payments? Suddenly at risk.

A Real World Example: The Budget That Bled Out

A borrower brought us a deal in Jacksonville, Florida. Solid neighborhood, good block construction, decent comps. The plan was to turn a dated rental into a clean, market-ready home. Rick (the borrower) bought the property for $205,000 and budgeted $65,000 for renovations, aiming for an ARV of $320,000.

The scope looked reasonable: new roof, updated kitchen and baths, new windows and doors, flooring throughout, and fresh paint inside and out. But two weeks into the project, the problems started.

First came water damage under the old vinyl flooring. Cue the mold remediation and subfloor replacement. Then the contractor discovered outdated plumbing that wasn't up to code. Then the HVAC died. Every week, a new problem—and a new expense.

By the time the dust settled, the rehab cost had ballooned from $65,000 to $92,000. That pushed the borrower's all-in cost to $297,000, leaving just a sliver of margin—and that's before accounting for interest payments, resale commissions, and closing costs.

We got repaid without the borrower coming out of pocket, but it was close. Too close.

The takeaway? If a deal only works when everything goes perfectly, it doesn't work. Never assume the initial budget is gospel.

As a private lender, your job isn't to strap on a tool belt or pick our backsplash tile. It's to vet the deal *before* the first nail is driven. If the rehab budget looks too tight, don't ignore the signal. Dig deeper. Ask tough questions. Because if the borrower can't control their rehab costs, you could lose control of your return.

Deal Killer #3: The Rehab Takes Longer Than Expected

Time is money. In private lending, that's not a cute saying—it's your business model. Every loan you fund ties up capital: the longer that capital stays locked in a deal, the slower your velocity, the fewer opportunities you can seize, and the harder it gets to stack and compound returns.

(Yes, you can mitigate this with a well-structured loan—and it's a surprisingly learnable skill—but we'll get to that later.)

This is why dragged-out rehabs are deal-killers.

Remember, private lending is a short-term game. And it only works if your borrower gets that too. A flip that should take five months but drags into twelve doesn't just stall your returns—it ratchets up your risk. The borrower's holding costs stack. He loses steam. His ability to execute erodes.

And let's not forget the market. A lot can change in seven months—and not always in your favor.

Why Rehab Timelines Slip (and How to Spot It Early)

These days, rehabs get delayed for all kinds of reasons:

- **Sometimes, it's contractors.** Even the "good" ones are juggling five jobs, showing up when they feel like it, and pushing timelines when they get stretched too thin. If your borrower doesn't have a system to keep them on task, that's not just a headache. It's a liability.

- **Other times, it's the supply chain.** Cabinets, flooring, appliances—stuff that used to show up in days can now take weeks or months. Sure, some delays just can't be helped. But a smart flipper knows that, and plans accordingly. They pre-order. They stage. They don't let their flip grind to a halt waiting on baseboards.

- **And sometimes the borrower just isn't ready.** No team lined up. No materials secured. No structured rehab timeline. They found the deal, but didn't put in the groundwork. Now the clock is ticking—on your capital.

"Your job as a private lender isn't to swing a hammer or pick out paint colors, it's to make sure the numbers make sense."

A Real World Example: The Long and Winding Rehab

A flipper in St Petersburg, FL brought us a deal in late 2021. Great spread on paper—$110K purchase price, $64K rehab, $240K ARV. The flipper was experienced, confident, and already had a contractor lined up. Seemed like a solid bet.

Then the delays started.

First, the contractor took on another job mid-project. "Just a week or two behind," he said. That turned into six. Then the kitchen cabinets got backordered—twice. The flipper hadn't ordered them in advance. By the time they were installed, the spring/summer selling season was over.

What should've been a four-month flip slogged into seven. Holding costs ate into the flipper's profits. And the comps that supported the ARV? Gone. Buyer demand had cooled thanks to Fed rate hikes and the usual seasonal drop-off, and prices softened.

For a buy-and-hold investor, that might be acceptable. For a flipper or private lender, it's just not.

Look, a great flip isn't just about getting the numbers right—it's about getting them right *quickly*. **The less time the project takes, the lower the holding costs, the higher the efficiency, and the faster your capital moves on to the next deal.**

If your borrower's timeline is shaky, walk away. The best deals are the ones that keep your money moving—and your returns stacking.

Deal Killer #4: The Estimated ARV (After Repair Value) is Too High

After Repair Value (ARV) is just what it sounds like: an estimate of what the house will resell for after the rehab is done.

And in flipping and private lending, everything hinges on ARV.

Why? Because, in most deals, the exit strategy is a flip: the borrower renovates the property, sells it at a higher price, and cashes out. That's when you get your principal back, along with any final interest owed (beyond the monthly interest you've been getting throughout the deal).

But what if your borrower doesn't get the price they want?

What if they were banking on $400,000, but the market says $350,000 at best? Suddenly all their numbers are shot. Their profit vanishes. Now they're stuck in a deal they can't exit without taking a haircut. If they won't drop price and eat the loss, you could end up trapped in a drawn-out mess that puts your principal at risk.

Of the 5 deal killers, this is the deadliest.

ARV Depends On The Three Types of Appreciation

There are three ways a property gains value in a flip:

- *Instant* **Appreciation** – Buying below market value from the jump. If a house is worth $300,000 as-is and your borrower locks it up for $270,000, they've already built in a $30,000 cushion. That's instant appreciation—value captured on day one.

- *Forced* **Appreciation** – Value added through renovations. A $20,000 kitchen upgrade may bump the resale price by $40,000 or more. That's strategic value creation. The flipper has *forced* appreciation by increasing the value of the home beyond the cost to do so.

- **Market Appreciation** – The catch-all wildcard: the increase (or decrease) in property values due to broader economic trends, supply and demand shifts, interest rates, and timing. It's by far the most unpredictable and least controllable of the three.

The final resale price—the ARV—depends on the whole trio.

If your borrower gets the ARV wrong (especially all three pieces), their profit shrinks fast. In some cases, it disappears altogether.

(Important note: that doesn't necessarily mean your return goes out the window. If the borrower has sufficient cash reserves and you built in the right cushion, your capital is still well protected.)

Why ARV Mistakes Are the #1 Deal Killer

A missed ARV is worse than overpaying on the purchase price. Worse than underestimating rehab costs. Even worse than a rehab dragging on for months.

Why?

Because your borrower can survive those other mistakes.

- If they overpay by $10,000 on acquisition, they can tighten up their rehab budget or ride an appreciating market.
- If the rehab goes over by $15,000, those extra improvements may translate into a higher-than-expected final resale price.
- If it takes a few extra months to sell, the holding costs sting— but rising prices during those months can soften the blow.

But if they screw up the ARV—if they think they'll sell for $400,000 but comps say $350,000 max—they're potentially dead in the water.

"As a private lender, your best defense is diligence."

Think about it: the resale price is the *single largest number* in the profit equation. Miss it by even a small percentage, and everything else collapses.

Let's use 10%. If you're off by 10% on a $60,000 rehab, that's $6,000 lost. Painful—but survivable.

Off by 10% on a $400,000 ARV? That's $40,000 gone. Enough to erase the flipper's entire profit.

And when the profit's gone, your risk spikes. Because if the borrower can't resell profitably, how do you get paid back?

How to Protect Yourself—In Advance

As a private lender, your best defense is diligence.

- Stick to bread-and-butter flips—homes in high-demand neighborhoods with strong comps and predictable resale values. Avoid quirky one-offs in soft or speculative markets.
- Verify the borrower's ARV assumptions. Don't take their word for it. Run your own comps: use recent sales, same square footage, same lot size, same planned upgrades. Dig in.
- Check days on market (DOM). If similar properties are sitting for months, your borrower's ARV or resale timeline might be fantasy.
- Above all, stay conservative. If the borrower says the home will resell for $400K, but comps point to $375K–$390K? Underwrite to $375K. Hope for the upside, but don't bet on it.

At the risk of repeating myself: when the ARV is off, everything else falls apart. The profit evaporates. The borrower often checks out, mentally and emotionally. And your repayment? It's suddenly at risk—unless you structured the deal to protect you.

That's why nothing matters more than this: the deal has to sell predictably, at the right price. Or it's not a deal at all.

Deal Killer #5: The Property Takes Too Long to Sell

A great deal moves fast.

Let's say your borrower nails the ARV estimate. The market agrees. Buyers show up. Offers roll in. The property closes at or above the projected price, and everyone gets paid.

That's how it's supposed to work.

But what if it doesn't?

What if the listing goes live...and crickets?

No showings. No offers. Just a property sitting stale while your capital stays locked—earning interest, yes, but dragging on far longer than expected.

In private lending, time is a double-edged sword. It can work for you—if the deal is structured properly—or slowly strangle your returns.

If a flip isn't selling, one of two things went wrong:

1. The borrower miscalculated the ARV.
    o   They thought they could sell for $325,000.
    o   The market says $290,000 max.
    o   Buyers smell the mispricing and don't bite.

2. The market shifted mid-flip.
   - Interest rates spiked.
   - A recession hit.
   - Buyer demand softened, and now houses are sitting longer across the board.

Why Sluggish Exits Kill Returns

Even if you're collecting interest, a delayed exit drags down your velocity of capital: the rate at which you can recycle your money into new deals within the same year.

Remember: **in private lending, the goal isn't just return *on* capital. It's return *of* capital. The faster you get your principal back, the faster you can redeploy it**—racking up new *origination fees*, boosting your annual ROI, and reducing your market exposure (bonus points for that one).

But when that timeline slips, so does your math. If, say, your borrower promised a six-month turnaround but now needs nine? Your projected annual yield just took a hit.

"The goal in private lending isn't just return on capital —it's return of capital."

And here's the bigger risk: the longer a property sits on the market, the worse it looks to buyers. They start wondering what's wrong with it. Showings slow down. A price cut becomes inevitable.

Suddenly, your borrower's margin shrinks—and so does your repayment confidence.

How to Spot the Risk Early

A few extra minutes of due diligence before you fund the deal can save you months of frustration later.

- **Verify Days on Market (DOM).** If similar properties are selling in 10 days, great. If they're sitting for 90+ days, that's a problem.

- **Check price trends.** Is the market stable? Climbing? Sliding? If values are dropping, you need to build that into your risk assessment.

- **Look at liquidity.** Are similar homes getting multiple offers, or collecting dust and price cuts? If demand is soft, your borrower may struggle to exit.

- **Stick to proven markets.** Unique homes in quirky neighborhoods might make good HGTV episodes—but they make terrible loan candidates. You want "down the fairway" flips in zip codes buyers are actually buying in.

A slow exit isn't just frustrating—it's costly. Your borrower's economics get squeezed from basically every direction, and yours start to look a lot less certain.

As a private lender, you're not just funding deals. You're funding deals that *sell*. If a deal can't exit cleanly, it was never that good to begin with.

Beyond the Deal Killers: The Real Edge Is Structure

Any one of these five blunders—overpaying, budget blowouts, timeline drags, ARV misses, or sluggish exits—can derail a deal, crush your borrower's profits, and hold your capital hostage.

But now? Now you know what to look for. That alone puts you miles ahead of most first-time lenders. While others learn through battle scars and write-offs, you're stepping in with clarity, caution, and an eye pre-trained to spot red flags.

Still, sniffing out a bad deal is just the first layer of defense.

If you want to build real confidence—and a portfolio that runs like clockwork—you need more than deal-killer awareness. You need strategy. Systems. A structured process that protects you and your money and guides every lending decision you make.

But don't worry, I've got you covered. I've got two pieces of structure right here to get you going.

First, a free eBook: *The 10 Commandments of Private Lending*. It's the field guide I wish I had when we started. Inside, you'll find the 10 unbreakable rules that keep your money safe, your returns consistent, and your stress level near zero.

It's 100% pure value, no fluff. Pages and pages worth. Download it using the QR code below and keep it close. You'll be glad you did.

Second, the next chapter. Beyond rules to live by, you also need your own decision-making playbook: your personal credit policy. A framework for quickly evaluating deals and borrowers—tailored to your goals, your risk tolerance, and your view of the world.

In the next chapter, we'll build that from the ground up. You'll walk away with a crystal-clear lens for vetting every deal that crosses your desk. That's a promise.

Because the best private lenders don't chase returns—they engineer them. They structure deals to win even if the deal itself is not a winner.

And many of our best deals? The ones we never did.

To get your copy of The 10 Commandments of Private Lending, visit www.justbethebank.com/commandments or scan the QR code below:

CHAPTER 7

Every Lender Needs a Credit Policy

"Beautiful credit! The foundation of modern society."
- Mark Twain

People love to say that money makes the world go 'round. But that's not quite true.

It's *credit* that keeps everything moving. Other People's Money.

And as a private lender, you can't afford to be casual about who gets yours. Just because you *have* capital doesn't mean you should deploy it into every shiny deal that lands in your inbox.

Selectivity is the name of the game. Holding out for grade-A deals. Making sure your money works for *you*—not the other way around.

The best way to do that?

Have a credit policy.

Think of your credit policy as your *private lending gospel*: a personalized set of non-negotiables that spell out exactly what deals you'll fund, under what terms, and where your hard stops live. Without one, you're flying blind; relying on gut feeling (or worse, the borrower's sales pitch), instead of a structured framework to assess risk and engineer returns.

See, if there's one thing my family learned from the subprime meltdown of 2008—and more recently, the implosion in commercial real estate—it's this: discipline wins.

The investors who had clear lending criteria and stuck to them? They survived. Many even thrived.

The ones who got loose with their standards?

Wiped out.

Your credit policy is your filtering system. It's what the thrivers use to screen out the garbage before it ever hits your balance sheet. A smart credit policy cuts through all the noise so you can zero in on *fewer, bette*r deals—ones that match your risk tolerance, capital availability, and long-term goals.

And here's the best part: this isn't rocket science. You don't need a finance degree or a team of underwriters to build a credit policy. In this chapter, I'll walk you through the key questions and decision points that shape a bulletproof policy—and I'll show you where to get even more insights to refine it for your network, your market, and your mission.

Because in private lending, the biggest mistakes don't come from saying "yes."

They come from not saying "no."

A Question-Based Approach to Establishing Your Credit Policy

Traditional lenders live and die by rigid, one-size-fits-all rules. They'll flat-out refuse loans under $100,000. They won't touch borrowers with credit scores below 650. Their policies are etched in stone, passed down from boardroom overlords who've never set foot on a job site.

But private lenders? We don't have to play that game. We get to be flexible. Personal. Strategic.

And that's exactly why we need structure. **Flexibility without a playbook is at best inconsistent. At worst it's chaos—sometimes, expensive chaos.**

The key here is to build a framework that protects your capital without killing your adaptability. A system with room to maneuver—but firm guardrails to keep you from veering off a cliff. The goal isn't rigidity, it's repeatability.

That's where a question-based approach comes in.

A static checklist is worthless. Instead, I use a series of guiding questions to shape (and reshape) my credit policy as conditions change. This question-based approach brings clarity and control, no matter what the market throws at you.

"Your credit policy is your personal private lending gospel."

The questions I'm about to lay out aren't random; they're forged from real deals, real dollars, and real consequences. They've been battle-tested across years of lending and more than 10,000 loans. These are the exact same filters we teach in our workshop to help investors spot winning deals fast, sidestep risk, and juice their returns.

I'll keep things high-level for now. But as you go through each question, let it marinate. Think about how it fits your investing lens—whether you're already lending or still gearing up to place your first bet.

What Is Your Loan Amount Range?

Before you write your first check, you need to define your strike zone—the loan size that fits your comfort level and your strategy. This isn't just about numbers. It's about *focus*.

And if you decide to broker loans to others (say, if your funds are limited or non-existent), the same principle applies. You'll want to ask your capital partners the magic question: **"How much do you want to lend per deal?"**

Now ask yourself the same thing. Are you aiming to diversify—spreading capital across multiple smaller loans to lower your risk? Or do you want to concentrate—fewer, bigger deals with bigger checks coming in?

Here's an example. A newer lender approached me after a conference I spoke at back in 2018. He said he was working with about $500,000, but from his story, it was clear he hadn't set a loan amount range. He'd jumped on a $460,000 loan in California—big project, long rehab, 9.25% interest—referred by a broker.

"At first," he said, "It felt like a win. I'd deployed almost all my capital in one shot. But a few weeks later, higher-paying deals (12–13%) started popping up in my local market in St. Louis. Smaller loans, quicker flips."

The FOMO was strong. Now he was at the conference trying to sell the California note just to free up liquidity and get in on the local action.

A little forethought on loan sizing could've saved him the scramble.

Your loan amount range is a direct reflection of your capital base, your risk appetite, and your deal-flow bandwidth. Some private lenders thrive making a dozen $50,000 loans at once. Others prefer just two or three carefully selected six-figure plays per year.

There's no wrong answer—just the one that aligns with your investing thesis.

Once you define your range, you've got your first built-in filter. You'll stop wasting time on mismatched deals. Every opportunity you evaluate will fit your bandwidth, your cash reserves, and your personal risk profile.

So start here: What's your number?

Because everything else builds on that.

What Is Your Loan Term Range?

How long are you willing to have your money tied up? That's the heart of this question.

Private lending is a short-term game—always has been, in our case. **Most deals land somewhere between 6 and 12 months**, though some wrap up in just a few weeks. Unlike banks that love locking up capital for 30 years, private lenders win by moving fast: get in, get paid monthly, get paid off, and redeploy.

Your loan term sweet spot depends on a few key factors:

- **Market Conditions:** There are market cycles and geographic markets. In uncertain market cycles, shorter terms reduce your exposure. But in strong, appreciating geographic markets—especially when profit shares are involved—longer timelines might work in your favor.

- **Capital Velocity:** How many times do you want to turn your money in a year? More turns equals more fees and more compounding.

- **Involvement Level:** Fast cycles require more hands-on attention. If you're looking for something closer to set-it-and-forget-it, longer-term loans might be your style.

Some lenders love the churn: shorter deals, faster flips, more profits. Others prefer a more relaxed pace, opting for fewer loans and longer timelines.

Again, there's no universal right answer here—only the right answer for you. But once you lock that in, you'll have more than just another filter; you'll have an investment rhythm that fits your life.

What's Your Geographic Boundary?

Where are you willing to put your money to work?

For many private lenders, **starting local makes the most sense.** You know the streets. You know which neighborhoods are rising, which are stagnating, and which zip codes should come with a warning label. You can drive by a property, talk to investors in person, and get a feel for the market in real time.

But it's not the only way to play The Money Game.

Some lenders go multi-market—or even nationwide—because they've built trusted boots-on-the-ground teams or have deep insight into other metros. Others expand strategically to diversify and reduce concentration risk.

Then there's the hybrid approach: lend close to home by default, but stay open to exceptional deals elsewhere. Maybe you decide you'll only lend within a 30-mile radius of your home, but if a trusted, repeat borrower brings you a no-brainer deal in another state, you'll consider it.

It's all about knowing your boundary. So ask yourself: **Are you comfortable evaluating deals from 2,000 miles away? Or do you want to be close enough to walk the property if something feels off?**

Your credit policy should make that decision for you. That way, when a deal hits your inbox, you're not guessing. You already know if it fits—or it doesn't.

Which Real Estate Categories Will You Lend On?

Every private lender needs a lane. What's yours?

Most real estate lending falls into three broad categories: residential, commercial, and industrial. Sure, you *could* try to play in all three— but **smart lenders specialize.** Specialization gives you an edge. It lets you learn the nuances, spot the traps, and seize the opportunities faster than anyone else in your niche.

Once you've picked your lane, you can drill down further:

- If it's commercial, are you after large office buildings or neighborhood retail strips?

- If it's industrial, are you into light manufacturing hubs near airports—or big-box logistics warehouses on major shipping routes?

- If it's residential, are you focused on single-family homes, duplexes, or small multifamily properties?

Let me give you a quick example: I know a lender who funded a light industrial deal—a small warehouse outside Dallas. On the surface, it checked all the right boxes: strong borrower, decent price, clear upside. But what he didn't factor in were the headaches that came with the subcategory.

Midway through the flip, zoning issues cropped up. Turns out the county had shifted regulations on small-bay warehouses, and the building needed upgrades to meet new codes before it could be leased or resold. What was supposed to be a 9-month deal turned into a 17-month capital freeze—and a lot of sleepless nights.

After that, he made a new rule: if he didn't fully understand the subcategory—and the risks baked into it—he wasn't funding it.

Personally, I've always stuck with residential—specifically single-family homes. Why? Because demand never goes away. People always need places to live, and single-family homes are the most liquid assets in any market cycle.

Your answer will depend on your background, your instincts, and your appetite for risk. What do you know? What kind of deals do you trust yourself to underwrite? Which asset class actually excites you?

Figure that out, and your lending strategy really starts to take shape.

What Borrower Experience Levels Will You Accept?

Not all borrowers are created equal. Some are battle-tested pros with a portfolio of successful exits. Others? They just binged a half dozen HGTV episodes and decided they're the next Chip and Joanna Gaines.

So—who do you want to lend to?

Technically, you *can* lend to anyone with a pulse and a property. But should you?

Here's my take: especially **in the beginning, stick with seasoned operators—flippers who've actually been in the trenches.** Experience lowers your risk. Veteran borrowers have managed contractors, survived budget blowouts, navigated delays, and still come out profitable. They don't just know how to start a project—they know how to finish it.

"Pick the right borrowers, and your lending business runs like a well-oiled machine."

The simplest way to vet them? Ask this:

"How many exits have you had in the last 12 months?"

An exit is a completed flip: bought, renovated, and resold for a profit. The more recent and frequent, the better.

- Zero? Red flag.

- One or two? Maybe—*if* they check other boxes.

- Five or more? Now we're talking.

Because here's the truth: you're not in the business of funding someone's real estate education. You're in the business of getting paid back—on time, with interest.

As I've told my sons: no one experiments with my money.

Pick the right borrowers, and your lending operation hums. Pick the wrong ones, and you're chasing down late payments and explaining to your spouse why your capital's trapped inside a half-gutted kitchen in the boonies.

Choose wisely.

Which applies to more than just lending, doesn't it?

What's the Base Price for Your Capital?

Now for the good stuff. How much are you charging for your money?

Your base price is your floor—the minimum interest rate you're willing to accept. Unlike banks, you're not shackled to the Fed's mood swings or arbitrary benchmarks. You set your price based on your market, your risk tolerance, and your borrower's track record.

You can go fixed—just one base rate for everyone. I wouldn't, but you can.

The better option is to be dynamic with your base; offering preferred rates to pros, and charging more for rookies with something to prove.

Here's the golden rule: charge what your capital *deserves* to earn.

And don't flinch at double-digit rates. A 10-12% return might sound steep compared to Wall Street's 6% "average," but guess what?

Your borrowers don't care.

They're not shopping for the cheapest money. They're shopping for speed, flexibility, and certainty.

If a bank *were* willing to fund a flip (which they're usually not), it would take weeks of paperwork, underwriters, committee approvals—and even then, it's a coin toss.

You? You can greenlight the deal in 24 hours and fund it in a week.

That's not just capital—it's oxygen. It's momentum. It's a shot at their next big payday.

So set your rates accordingly. You're not selling money. You're selling opportunity.

What Are Your Loan-to-Cost and Loan-to-Value Ratios?

Here's where private lending shifts from art...to cold, hard math.

Two numbers rule the game:

- **Loan-to-Cost (LTC):** How much of the *acquisition price* (for the house itself) are you willing to fund?

- **Loan-to-Value** (**LTV**): How much of the *after-repair value* (ARV) will your loan represent?

Both are about one thing: protecting your downside.

Because if you lend too much, guess what? Your borrower has no real skin in the game. And when someone's not personally invested, they're way more likely to cut and run the moment things get tough.

You never want to be the last one standing when the music stops.

I know a lender who funded a deal at 72% LTV—not bad, not great—but also 100% LTC. No down payment, in other words. No borrower cash on the line.

At first, everything seemed on track. But a few months in, the borrower's wife filed for divorce. He was so distraught and distracted he simply walked away from the project. With no cash invested, he didn't have much reason to fight for the deal.

It wasn't a total catastrophe; the lender was able to recover the property through a quitclaim deed and finish the flip himself. But after that mess, he made a new rule: no matter how good the numbers look, the borrower has to bring real money to the table. Period.

We live by the same rule. **We require borrowers to pony up at least 10-20% of the acquisition price—real cash, wired at closing.** Not just sweat equity. Not just good intentions.

And on the LTV side? We keep it tight: 60–70% of the ARV, max.

Meaning if the flipper says the property will sell for $400,000 post-renovation, we'll cap our total loan—purchase plus rehab—at $240,000 to $280,000.

Why? Because that cushion buys you time. It buys you options. It buys you peace of mind against overestimated resale prices, market shifts, or project delays.

At the end of the day, your LTC and LTV numbers aren't suggestions. They're your safety net.

If a deal can't clear those bars, it's not a deal worth doing.

What Will Your Origination Fees Be?

Origination fees—better known as "points"—are how you get paid upfront.

If your interest rate is what your *capital* is worth to you, points are what your *time and effort* are worth to you.

Every loan takes some initial work. You review the deal. Vet the borrower. Underwrite the numbers. Pull together the legal docs. It's not a heavy lift—but it's not nothing, either. And that effort deserves to be compensated *before* your money even leaves the station.

How do points work?

One "point" equals 1% of the loan amount.

So if you lend $200,000, a 2-point origination fee means you collect $4,000—wired to you at closing, before the borrower touches a dime of your capital.

"Origination fees—better known as "points"—are how you get paid upfront."

Smart private lenders always collect points upfront. Why?

- **It locks in immediate profit.** Even if the deal goes sideways, you've already been paid.

- **It filters out broke borrowers.** If they can't scrape together the points, they have no business flipping houses.

- **It rewards your effort.** Your time isn't free, and your expertise isn't either.

How many points should you charge?

It depends on the market, the borrower, and the risk. Somewhere between 1-4 points is standard. For riskier deals—less experienced borrowers, shaky markets, soft comps—charge at the higher end. For rock-solid deals in strong markets? Maybe you shave it down to stay competitive.

Net-net: **points aren't an add-on: they're part of your business model. Charge what your time and expertise are worth.**

What Scope of Work Are You Comfortable Financing?

Flips come in all shapes and sizes—and not all of them are created to make you money. Some are quick, cosmetic jobs. Others are serious construction projects.

Your job as a private lender? Know which ones you're willing to fund—before you bite off more than you can chew.

When we say "scope of work" here, we're referring to the general scale of renovation your borrower plans to tackle. Here's the rough spectrum:

- **Lipstick-and-Rouge Jobs** – Light renovations: paint, flooring, fixtures, cabinets, appliances. Quick turnarounds, fewer surprises, lower risk.

- **Mid-Tier Renovations** – Bigger lifts: new kitchens, bathrooms, HVAC replacements, roofing, moderate layout changes. Longer timelines, but still manageable if planned well.

- **Gut Jobs & Structural Overhauls** – Full transformations: knocking down walls, adding square footage, foundation repairs, mold remediation. These can drag for months—and the ways to go over budget are endless.

Which type should you fund?

It comes down to your risk appetite and experience.

Cosmetic flips? Lower risk. Faster exits. More predictable cash flow.

Gut jobs? Bigger potential profits—but far bigger unknowns, and way more things that can derail a deal (and your returns).

A quick real-life example: a broker we know had a flipper who got lured into a structural rehab in Marietta, GA. Looked like a $90K profit on paper. Six months later, the flipper was in permit hell with a slab foundation issue. Took 14 months to exit and they barely broke even. That deal taught them the difference between "opportunity" and "overreach."

Here's a simple rule of thumb:

If a project needs blueprints, multiple permits, or a structural engineer, it's a whole different ballgame. Lenders who fund those kinds of deals usually have experience, deep pockets, and a lot of patience—and they price their risk accordingly.

Bottom line: know your lane. Stick to projects that match your comfort zone—and don't let a flipper's overconfidence become your problem.

What Credit Scores and Backgrounds Are You Willing to Finance?

In private lending, you're not just funding deals—you're funding people.

Deals don't do deals, people do deals.

And while real estate tends to follow predictable patterns, people can be wildcards. That's why smart lenders draw a hard line when it comes to borrower credit scores and backgrounds.

First, credit scores.

A surprising number of lenders take the fog-a-mirror approach; they'll fund anyone with a pulse. That's a fast track to stress. Setting a minimum FICO score gives you an automatic filter—one that saves time and screens out borrowers who can't even manage their own financial lives.

Where you draw that line is up to you. Some lenders won't touch anyone under 650. Others might flex lower—*if* the deal is rock-solid and heavily collateralized.

But the lower you go, the more risk you take—and the more risk premium (higher rates and fees) you should demand in return.

Now, what about borrower backgrounds?

- Are you comfortable lending to first-time flippers?

- What about someone with a past bankruptcy—or a foreclosure?

- Are prior felonies a dealbreaker? (They are for me.)

- How about life events like divorce—red flag, or just life happening?

I'm not saying your borrower has to be perfect. But they *do* have to be predictable.

Because when you lend, you're entering into a financial relationship. The question is: Is the borrower *worthy* of that relationship?

Are they stable, disciplined, and trustworthy enough to handle your money—or are they a walking financial grenade, just waiting to explode?

Some private lenders will tell you it's all about the collateral—the house, the deal—not the borrower. But I don't subscribe to that. If someone's past is littered with unpaid bills, broken contracts, or legal battles, what makes you think they're going to pay you your 12% interest when life inevitably throws them a curveball?

Sure, you *could* foreclose and take the property back. But now you're a flipper. And trust me: the effort-to-return ratio for flipping houses doesn't come close to private lending. (It's not even in the same galaxy.)

Commit this to memory: choose your borrowers like you'd choose a business partner. Set your standards, stick to them, and never let someone else's desperation become your risk.

Live By Your Credit Policy... and Keep Learning

If you've been skimming this chapter, I get it. Private lending is a big topic. And until it feels real—until you're staring down an actual deal—you might not be hanging on every word.

But trust me on this: the moment you're about to put real money on the line, this credit policy stuff becomes your lifeline.

Your goal isn't just to say "yes" to good deals…
It's to say "no" to the wrong ones as quickly as possible.

The faster you filter out the crap, the more time you have to find (and fund) the gold. **Your credit policy is the way you do it. It's your personal cheat sheet to keep your ROI high, your stress minimal, and your investment life fully under your control.**

Now, this chapter was necessarily high-level. With thousands of deals under our belt, our family office has taken every one of these questions ten layers deeper.

If you want to explore those layers and take your knowledge even further, good. I've got just the thing.

Head on over to justbethebank.com using the QR code below. There you'll find a set of free (but so good they feel paid) resources: guides, tools, and real-world case studies, all designed to help you sharpen your credit policy and turn your loan decision-making into a serious competitive advantage.

They're the kind of resources I wish I had when I started. And they're yours, free.

And keep in mind: whether or not you become a full-time lender, the insights you're gaining here will serve you for *life*—in real estate, in investing, and in every deal you ever do.

All that said, my favorite part about private lending—the part that still blows people's minds when I teach it in our workshops—is still ahead.

It's the fact that you can grow your capital completely tax-free.

It's one of the best-kept secrets in *The Money Game*. And in the next chapter, I'm pulling back the curtain.

Get ready. You're going to want to hear this.

To get your copy of The 10 Point Framework for a Bulletproof Lending Policy, visit www.justbethebank.com/creditpolicy or scan the QR code below:

CHAPTER 8

The Tax-Free Way to Do Private Lending

"I am proud to be paying taxes in the United States.
The only thing is - I could be just as proud
for half the money."
- Arthur Godfrey

If you're still not convinced that private lending is one of the greatest wealth-building tools out there, allow me to sweeten the pot.

What if I told you there's a way to turbocharge your lending returns? A way to take all the upside—the double-digit ROI, the control, the predictable cash flow—and strip away the biggest drag on any investment: the taxes?

It's not magic. It's not some shady loophole. It's 100% legal, fully backed by the U.S. tax code.

All you need are the right structures in place—and you'll keep more of what you earn, compounding your wealth at an entirely different level.

First, though, a disclaimer:

Seek professional advice, and listen to YOUR advisors.

Let's be clear: I'm not your financial planner. I'm not your CPA. I'm not your tax attorney. I don't know your specific financial situation, and I'm not here to give you personalized tax or investment advice.

What I can do is share what's worked for me—how I've legally structured tax-free private lending deals and how it's helped grow my family's wealth. But your circumstances are different from mine, and tax laws change.

So before you dive in, consult your own tax and financial professionals. Have them review your situation, run the numbers, and confirm that any strategy you pursue aligns with your goals and keeps you on the right side of the IRS.

This chapter is meant to open your eyes to what's possible—not to replace expert guidance. Be smart. Do your due diligence. And always follow the advice of the professionals you trust.

With that out of the way—if you're serious about keeping more of your profits, compounding your capital faster, and building generational wealth legally, you're right where you need to be.

In the pages ahead, I'll break down:

- How I stumbled onto tax-free private lending—and why it changed the way I invest forever.
- The key financial structures you need to make it work.
- How our family has already used this strategy to maximize wealth across three generations.

- How you can apply these principles to build a financial-freedom foundation for yourself, your children, and even your grandchildren.

And at the center of it all? A retirement savings vehicle you may have heard of—but probably aren't using anywhere close to its full potential.

How I Took Control of My Retirement Funds (and Nuked Wall Street's Grip)

Back in my corporate days, I had one hard-and-fast rule when it came to money: max out my retirement accounts every single year. It was drilled into me, the way it's drilled into every working American—the gospel of 401(k)s and IRAs, the so-called golden ticket to a cushy retirement.

I guarantee you've heard the same advice. *Stuff as much money as possible into those accounts. Let it grow tax-deferred or tax-free. One day, decades from now, you'll cash in.*

That's the story they sell you, anyway.

The problem? **With traditional 401(k)s and IRAs—whether tax-deferred (traditional, SEP, etc.) or tax-free (Roth)—your investment choices are nil.** Your money gets funneled straight into the stock market. Surprise, surprise: that's exactly what Wall Street wants.

And sure, sometimes it works out. But when markets tank, when corrections hit, when entire sectors get wiped out overnight, guess what?

Nobody's making you whole.

When Merrill Lynch torched $250,000 of my retirement savings, I didn't get a refund. I didn't get a do-over. I didn't even get a return phone call. I just had to eat the loss. Decades of disciplined savings, chewed up by a system where I had zero control over the outcome.

That, my friends, is a rigged game. And yet, the financial industry expects you to shrug it off, keep contributing, and trust them to do better next time.

Yeah. No thanks.

For me, that was unacceptable. But strangely enough, *I'm glad I took that beating.*

I remember hearing Tony Robbins say that people only do anything for one of two reasons: to avoid pain or to gain pleasure.

Well, watching Merrill Lynch turn my 401(k) into a 201(k)—that was pain. Torture, even. A truly brutal lesson carved into my financial DNA.

But it *was* a lesson. One half of my "wins and lessons" (never wins and losses) philosophy. Now I just needed a *win*.

The first win was simple: asking a better question. As in, *if Wall Street's rigged against me, how do I invest in what I want—and never hand control to a broker again?*

A pretty decent question, I thought.

And it wasn't long before I got my answer.

The Day I Discovered Tax-Free Lending

I first heard about it at a REIA meeting in San Diego. One of the featured speakers was talking about retirement accounts, and my ears perked up.

"Most people don't realize this," he said, "but there's a type of retirement account you can use to invest in almost anything you want, tax free. It comes in both traditional and Roth flavors—IRA and 401(k)—but with one massive difference: you're in charge."

He called it a self-directed IRA (SDIRA).

I shot a skeptical look at the guy sitting next to me. "This can't be real," I whispered. "No way is this legal."

I mean, think about it: the idea that you could take retirement funds, rip them out of Wall Street's grip, and deploy them into high-ROI private deals—without paying taxes on the gains? It sounded like something a crackpot flat-earther might say.

But it turned out it wasn't. It *was* real. It *was* perfectly legal. And more than that, it was my ticket to stacking zeros onto my retirement account faster than Merrill Lynch ever could have—even if they hadn't torched half my savings.

And it's not like I was discovering some fringe loophole. Some of the world's savviest investors were already leveraging the crap out of SDIRAs.

Like Peter Thiel, big-boy venture capitalist and co-founder of PayPal. He put $2,000 in a Roth SDIRA back in 1999, and used it to buy shares of private, early-stage tech investments (including Facebook and PayPal itself).

Twenty years later, his account had grown to a cool $5 Billion. With zero taxes.

Of course, the brokerage industry doesn't want you to know that. They conveniently forget to mention SDIRAs at all—probably because it cuts them out of the equation. Surveys estimate that only 3-5% of American retirement accounts stray from the Wall Street herd, or even know they have the option to. Meaning 95% of people never realize they have a choice.

But you do. At least you do now.

To sum it up: with a traditional account, your options are limited to whatever dusty mutual funds your provider offers. Nuts to that.

With a SDIRA, you get freedom. Freedom to invest in real estate. Private equity. Crypto. A stud bull, if that's your thing. And most importantly for us: private lending.

Yes, you can use your SDIRA to become the bank, and do it on steroids.

If you value control over your financial future—and I'm guessing you do, since you're still reading—a SDIRA is a game-changer like no other. A legal, IRS-approved, tax-advantaged way to build walk-away wealth on your terms.

Master this, and you'll never look at retirement accounts, or your financial future, the same way again.

How This Became My Family's Generational Wealth Play

Once I accepted that SDIRAs were real—and not some tinfoil-hat fantasy—I had a decision to make: what would I actually *hold* inside my SDIRA? Real estate? Precious metals? Private equity?

Those were the obvious plays. A lot of investors default to real estate, and I get it. I love real estate as an asset class too, at the right point in the cycle.

But I decided early on that I didn't want to own physical property inside my SDIRA. Why?

Because physical property carries liability. One slip-and-fall lawsuit. One bad tenant. One property management disaster. Any one of these and my entire retirement account—everything I had fought to protect—could be exposed.

Private lending, on the other hand, is just paper. *Notes*, as we call them in the biz.

It's clean. Streamlined. No tenants. No evictions. No angry neighbors or midnight maintenance calls. Just capital in, capital out—and interest flowing back into my SDIRA, with Uncle Sam entitled to *nada*.

Control without chaos. Growth without drama. Wealth-building the way it should be.

Private lending didn't just give me an investment strategy, in other words. It gave me *peace of mind*.

So I had my asset class locked in. Next step: make it happen.

I took what was left after the Merrill Lynch debacle—a small six-figure sum that had somehow survived Wall Street's buffoonery—and rolled it into a Roth SDIRA. That was my seed capital.

And honestly, that one move changed everything.

It was the catalyst for my whole investing career. Everything you've been reading about in this book started there—the way my family and I structured our private lending business, how we scaled it to thousands of deals, and how we built a generational wealth machine. All because of that little Roth SDIRA conversion.

And my very first private lending deal? It happened inside that account.

Here's the kicker though: that money isn't just mine.

Say what? It's an *individual* retirement account, right?

Yes, but a Roth SDIRA doesn't just protect *your* capital. It protects your heirs' capital after you're gone, too. **If I got hit by a bus tomorrow, my Roth SDIRA would pass directly to my designated beneficiaries—yes, tax-free.**

Now, as I've said before, I'm not a tax attorney and I don't play one on TV. You'll want to confirm the current rules with your CPA or tax attorney. But under today's laws, inherited Roth IRAs come with a 10-year window before the beneficiary has to fully withdraw the funds.

Which means if my sons manage it wisely, they can keep compounding gains (still tax-free) for another full decade before ever touching the principal.

And if you remember our penny-doubling example, you already know what that means for long-term wealth creation. The longer you can keep money compounding—without interruption, without taxation, without drag—the bigger the snowball grows.

And the bigger the snowball, the bigger the legacy.

Funding Your Roth SDIRA

Roth IRAs and 401(k)s are unique beasts. You pay taxes on the money going in—but everything it earns from that point forward grows tax-free. Forever.

And when you take qualified withdrawals? Zero tax. No matter how much it's grown.

Then there's the contribution side: straightforward at first glance, but packed with loopholes once you know where to look.

In 2025, Roth IRA contributions are capped at $7,000 if you're under 50, or $8,000 if you're 50 or older. Simple enough, right?

Sure, simple at first glance. But peel back the layers, and you'll find an entire hidden world of Roth funding strategies the wealthy have quietly mastered.

Did you know that if you have an old 529 college savings plan—one that's been open for at least 15 years—you can roll some of it into a Roth? Or that you can convert a 401(k) into a Roth IRA, like I did when I first started?

"The longer you can keep your money compounding—without interruption, without taxation, without tax drag—the greater your ultimate wealth potential."

And what if you make too much money?

The IRS says if you earn over $145,000, you're locked out of contributing directly to a Roth IRA.

Enter the *backdoor Roth conversion*: a perfectly legal workaround that high-income earners use to unlock all the tax-free benefits of a Roth anyway.

Point being? There are more ways to fund a Roth than most people realize.

Get Help—This Is Way Too Important to Wing It

Look, tax law is no joke. One missed detail could cost you thousands—or worse, blow up the whole tax-free compounding advantage you're chasing.

If you're serious about using a self-directed traditional or Roth SDIRA for private lending, do yourself a favor: get professional guidance.

Start with a little homework. Head over to the IRS site: www.irs.gov/retirement-plans/roth-iras.

That'll give you just enough information to be dangerous—to start asking better questions. Then it's time to bring in the experts. Sit down with a trusted tax advisor or accountant who understands SDIRAs inside and out. And while you're at it, get a second opinion too. (Seriously.)

Why all the caution?

Because this isn't just about saving a few bucks on taxes.

It's about building a legally bulletproof fortress around your profits— and setting your wealth compounding on a whole different level.

Leveraging Roth SDIRAs to Build Wealth Across Generations

Imagine this: your kids or grandkids building tax-free wealth before they even graduate high school. Thanks to Roth SDIRAs, it's not just possible—it's the smartest financial head start you can give them.

Because time is the most powerful force in wealth-building. Hands down. The earlier you start, the bigger the numbers get.

All it takes is earned income. As long as they have that, your kids can open Roth self-directed retirement accounts—and start compounding tax-free, decades ahead of everyone else.

And it gets even better: kids can participate in private lending too.

They might not be able to sign contracts yet, but they can legally partner with adults—pooling their SDIRA contributions into loans and earning money tax-free right alongside you.

(Quick note: If you're using SDIRAs, there's one critical rule you can't afford to break—the "lineal descendants" rule. In plain English? Your SDIRA and your kid's SDIRA can't do business together. No lending. No co-investing. No creative loopholes. Cross that line, and the IRS will slap you with a "prohibited transaction"—bureaucrat-speak for a giant, costly headache you don't want.)

But the opportunity still stands. **Instead of letting your kids' early earnings languish in low-interest savings accounts (if they even have earnings), take charge. Help them generate earned income now, and put that money to work.**

Take Cooper. A dear friend of mine, and one of our Just Be the Bank workshop alumni. He didn't just teach his kids how to save a few bucks. He showed them how to be the bank.

Starting with money from a little side hustle—beekeeping, of all things—his kids parlayed their earnings into private lending deals alongside their dad. They've now planted the seeds of lifelong wealth, before most of their classmates even opened their first checking accounts.

(You can read more about Cooper's success at justbethebank.com/stories to see how he did it.)

The point? Your Roth SDIRA isn't just a tool for your financial freedom. It's a cornerstone for generational wealth.

And the sooner you put it in their hands, the stronger their foundation will be.

What 95% of Americans Don't Do... But You Will

The vast majority of Americans—95% or more—will never even consider using a self-directed Roth IRA. Even fewer will do private lending out of it. They won't take the time to understand it, won't explore the opportunities, and won't take action.

But that's not you.

As I always tell my sons, it's easy to be financially successful in America—because most people simply aren't *committed*.

See, commitment isn't just doing what you say you'll do.

Commitment is the promise that the conscious mind makes to the soul.

Before I commit to something—or someone—I think about it. If it's significant enough, I think about it *deeply*. Only then will I commit. Only then does it transfer from my head to my soul.

"Commitment is the promise that the conscious mind makes to the soul."

Because when you're committed, you find a way. When you're not, you find an excuse.

If you were content following the herd—blindly throwing your money into Wall Street's black hole—you wouldn't still be reading. You'd be checking your brokerage account once a quarter, hoping for the best while paying hidden fees to people who get rich at your expense.

Instead, you're here. You're choosing to learn how to take control of your money, extract maximum value from your capital, and legally keep Uncle Sam's hands out of your pocket.

This is how the uber-wealthy play The Money Game.

And it's not like it takes a lifetime of study. It doesn't take an MBA. It takes one decision: that you're no longer willing to leave your financial future to chance.

So now it's time to make that choice.

Do what 95% of people do—nothing.

Or take your first step toward becoming a private lender.

In the final chapters, I'll show you what it really looks like to get in the game—and start racking up W's. You'll see the smartest, lowest-friction ways to launch. How much capital you actually need (hint: it's less than you think). And how to skip the rookie phase entirely by doing what my sons did: inherit wisdom, shortcut mistakes, and start from someone else's finish line.

This is where it all starts to click.

Let's go.

CHAPTER 9

From One Deal to a Dynasty: Launching Your Private Lending Empire

"It's not how much money you make, but how much money you keep, how hard it works for you, and how many generations you keep it for."
- Robert Kiyosaki

Alright, now it's go time.

You've reshaped the way you see money. You've unlocked a strategy the ultra-high-net-worths have used for millennia. You've started thinking—and acting—like the bank.

You've also gotten tactical. Built your own credit policy. Learned to spot the five deal killers before they spot you. You even figured out how to cut Uncle Sam out of the equation, and bend the odds in your favor for good.

But here's the thing: knowledge alone won't change your financial future.

At some point, you have to pull the trigger. Because all the theory, all the best practices, all the insider strategies—none of that will make you a penny richer, or do a thing to improve your family's future, if you don't put them into play.

So let's do this. Let's start building your empire.

How Much Do You Need to Start Private Lending?

Capital. It's the first question on everyone's mind when they think about stepping into private lending. And rightfully so: this game is about making your money work for you, and that means you need some to start.

We've touched on capital throughout this book, but let's spell it out clearly: **you need enough to do one loan. Your first loan. Or your first loan with someone else's money.**

That's it. One deal, and you're in the business. No magic number, no secret formula. Just enough to fund a single, solid loan.

So how much is that? It depends on where you're lending (geographic market) and what category and subcategory you're lending on (residential; single-family home, duplex, etc).

In affordable residential markets, you might be looking at $50,000 or less to fund a deal. I know private lenders—successful ones—who've built their business with a self-imposed cap of $50K per loan and are thriving.

In a median-priced market, you might start at $100,000 or more. And if you're in a high-priced market like California, New York, or any major metro, your starting point will be higher.

It's the same real estate rule that governs everything else: location, location, location.

And remember, you don't have to go it alone. You can partner with financial friends—multiple lenders co-funding the same deal—to reduce your personal capital requirement.

Beyond your starting capital, your credit policy will guide how much you'll ultimately allocate to private lending. How many loans do you want to do at once? How quickly do you want your capital turning over? Do you want to stay lean with just a handful of high-return deals, or build a larger lending portfolio?

All of that comes later. For now, all you need is enough to do one loan. Either your first one or your next one.

Get in the game and get a deal done. Then what? You scale.

Play Smaller to Get Bigger

When I say "do one loan," I don't necessarily mean you fund it yourself outright. If you don't have the liquidity to do a whole loan (or any loan at all), there are still ways to dip your toe in, build capital, and grow into larger deals.

The two best paths? *Brokering* loans and *wrap* loans.

Brokering: Profit Without Putting Up a Dime

Brokering—essentially playing matchmaker—allows you to profit from private lending without putting up any of the capital yourself.

It's super simple: you connect borrowers who need funding with lenders who have the cash. In return, you get paid. Some brokers charge a flat fee just for making the connection. Others take a percentage of the deal or even secure a small piece of the loan itself—earning all or some of the origination fees or a point or two in ongoing interest.

You can run brokering as a full-time business or use it as a stepping stone to build your own capital base for independent lending. It's up to you.

Wrap Lending: The Power Move for Small Capital

Another strategy is the wrap loan.

This is where you contribute a smaller amount—say, 15-20% of the total loan—into a deal with another lender who contributes the balance. Your capital "wraps" around the larger loan, allowing you to participate without having to cover the full loan yourself.

Wrap loans are perfect for:

- People with smaller self-directed IRA or 401(k) balances who want to put their capital to work.
- Lenders who don't have immediate access to full liquidity but don't want to miss great deals.

- Families looking to build generational wealth by partnering parents, children, and grandchildren in thoughtfully structured loans.

How It Works: The Wrap Loan Breakdown

Any time I bring up wrap lending, people lean in. They get pretty fired up. And it's no mystery why—it's slick, creative, and one of the highest-leverage moves in the entire private lending playbook.

Say a borrower (let's call him Joe) needs a $150,000 loan. You've only got $25,000 in liquidity. Instead of walking away, you structure a wrap loan:

- You bring in an investor—Mike—who agrees to fund the remaining $125,000 at 8% interest and 1 point in origination fees.
- You, meanwhile, charge Joe 12% interest and 2 points on the full $150,000 loan.
- Your wrap loan "encloses" the senior loan, meaning Joe makes one payment to you of 12%, and you're responsible for paying Mike his agreed-upon annual 8%.
- The difference—4% interest and 1 extra point—goes straight into your pocket.

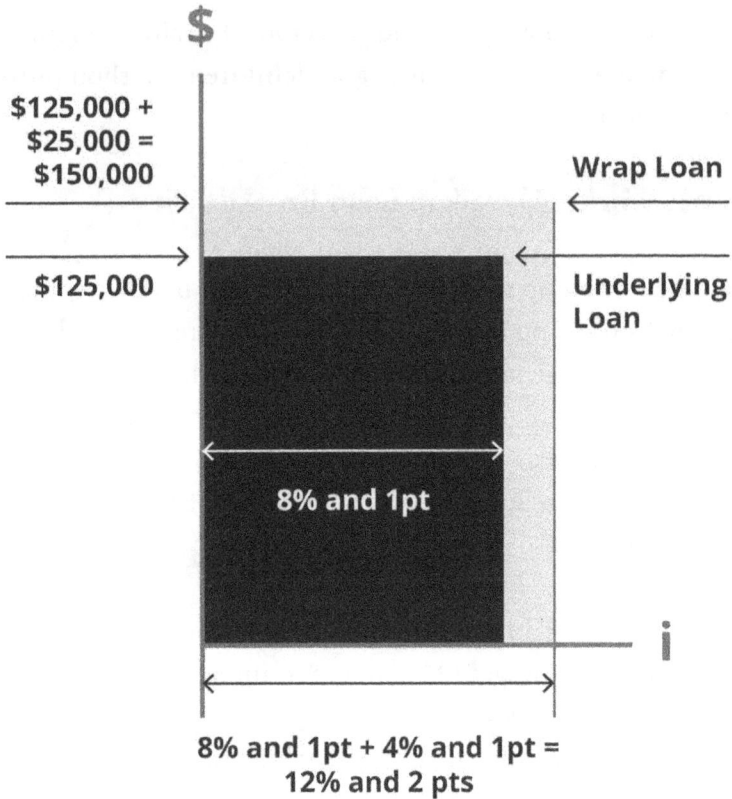

$125,000 +
$25,000 =
$150,000

Wrap Loan

$125,000

Underlying
Loan

8% and 1pt

8% and 1pt + 4% and 1pt =
12% and 2 pts

The proportions in the graphic aren't exact, but you get the point. You're *arbitraging* Mike's capital. **You're leveraging Other People's Money (OPM) to create a spread between what you charge the borrower and what you owe your investor.** And that spread? That's found money. Literally infinite return. Financial alchemy, but real.

And don't forget, on your own $25,000 contribution, you're earning the full 12% interest and 2 points. Stack it all up, and you're looking at truly phenomenal ROI numbers:

- You're getting 1 point and 4% on Mike's $125,000
- And 2 points and 12% on your $25,000

Blended together, your yield pencils out to 39%. On one 12-month deal.

Now, take it a step further. Imagine you did that deal inside an SDIRA—and just kept reinvesting your $25K principal and all your profits. You kept repeating the same type of deal, at the same rate of return, for 7 years straight.

You could 10X that account by the end of year 7…without ever adding another dollar of fresh capital.

Year	Starting Investment	Annual Profit	Year End Balance	# of $25K Deals/Year
1	$25,000	$9,750	$34,750	1.0
2	$34,750	$13,553	$48,303	1.4
3	$48,303	$18,838	$67,140	1.9
4	$67,140	$26,185	$93,325	2.7
5	$93,325	$36,397	$129,722	3.7
6	$129,722	$50,592	$180,314	5.2
7	$180,314	$70,322	$250,636	7.2

Let that sink in.

That's not some lottery-ticket, high-risk gamble. It's not a crypto moonshot or hoping for a unicorn startup. It's a calculated, repeatable strategy—built around secured loans, tight deal structures, and a beautiful little concept called arbitrage.

And yet, this is just one illustration. One example of what's possible for those who open their money lens and truly embrace what it means to be the bank.

Passing It Down: Wealth & Wisdom

Let's go even further. Take this same concept and imagine doing it for a child in your life. A son. A daughter. A grandkid. A niece or nephew just starting their first job.

Instead of handing them a check for college or setting them up with a brokerage account where their money rides Wall Street's rollercoaster, you show them a different way. You walk them through their first wrap loan. You open them up to a sharper money lens, show them the skill set you've honed, and help them deploy small amounts of capital into real deals.

And for the first time, they see money not as something to spend—but as something to grow.

"Grateful but not content."

At first, they might not fully grasp what you're doing for them. But give it time. When they see that money compound, when they see cash flow stacking up without punching a clock—when they realize that wealth is something you *build*, not *hope for*, that's when the real gift clicks into place.

You're not just handing them dollars. You're handing them knowledge. A way of thinking that most people will never learn.

I want you to internalize what I'm about to say next.

What you don't learn, your kids will inherit.

It's called Knowledge Arbitrage, and it's even more powerful than financial arbitrage. It's the form of leverage that great families value above everything else.

Because when you pass down wisdom, you're compounding every future generation's ability to win The Money Game.

My son Blake has arguably the most important job in our family. He builds and curates our Stech Family Legacy Library, where we've captured all our intellectual property—our collective wisdom—for subsequent generations to watch and learn from long after we're gone.

Meanwhile, Josh is building his next unicorn and investing in his growing family, just like I did at his age (minus the unicorn part).

My sons, and those after them, inspire me to keep doing what I do—even though I haven't had to work for a long time. Seriously, what kind of message would I be sending to my kids and grandkids if I retired? If I settled?

Instead, I wake up every day to the four words I wrote down 40 years ago in my cubicle in London, not far from where Blake was born.

Grateful but not content.

How Relationships Unlock Bigger Deals—and Bigger Money

No matter how much capital you start with, your network will dictate your ceiling.

In real estate—and especially in private lending—relationships are everything. They connect you to borrowers. They help you read market shifts before they happen. They introduce you to the real players: the ones actually doing deals, not just talking about them.

And most importantly, they open doors to bigger opportunities—and bigger money.

Because here's the truth: at some point, you're going to run out of your own capital to deploy. And the better you get at this, the faster it'll happen.

Even if you start with a healthy stack of cash, success in this business can create a strange problem: a liquidity crunch. Your money gets tied up in deals faster than they pay off, but the deals keep coming.

That's not a bad thing. It's the opposite. It's a positive forcing function—a clear sign that you're ready to scale.

In our early Vegas days, my sons and I ran out of money (my money) quickly. They were fresh out of Stanford and Berkeley, and broke. I was broker from putting them through school.

Between our modest starting capital and the outsized success we had early on, it wasn't long before I had to sit them down at our little office on Flamingo Road and break the news:

"We're out of money."

We had a choice to make—and we had to make it fast. Three options, I told them:

1. Stay small and keep it all.
2. Go big or go home.
3. Just add a zero.

Without hesitation, in perfect broke-twenty-something unison, they shouted: "Go big or go home!"

I smiled—and lowered the boom.

"I figured you'd say that. But here's the thing: You're young, you're broke, and you've got a lifetime ahead of you to bounce back if we crash and burn. I'm in my 50s—and I've got all the money in this. Which means... I have majority voting rights."

They groaned. I grinned.

"Congratulations," I said. "We're going to just add a zero. And when we add that one? We'll add another."

And that's exactly what we did.

Scaling Beyond Your Own Money (and My "Jerry Maguire" Epiphany)

This is where your network really kicks in.

When you hit that inflection point—where you've got great deals but not enough capital to fund them—you have two choices:

1. Go back to brokering or wrap lending to rebuild your purse, and keep playing small until you're ready to go big.
2. Leverage other people's money and start deploying capital at scale to add a zero.

Lending with OPM is the next evolution of private lending. It's how you stop playing with just your own money and start leveraging capital like the pros.

When we launched our first blind pool investment fund—raising capital from accredited investors—we weren't just deploying our own money anymore. We were *renting* capital. Arbitraging the spread. We were accelerating wealth-building in a way that simply wasn't possible when it was all on our backs.

I'm not saying you'll get there overnight. But if you build your network right, it's not a question of *if*. It's *when*.

And when that moment comes—when the right deal is staring you in the face—you won't be scrambling for capital.

You'll have the network. You'll have the resources. And you'll be ready to go big.

For us, our network-building started with a white paper I wrote in the middle of the night. A night I was so upset, I couldn't sleep. I called it my Jerry Maguire epiphany: **The Power of 6™**.

It changed everything—for me, for my sons, for our family's future. In ways I couldn't have dreamed possible.

From that eureka moment, I created our family mantra:

We Do Fewer Bigger Things with Fewer Better People
through Fewer Deeper Relationships.

We apply that mantra in everything we do, especially private lending.

The result? Thousands of deals. A portfolio that scaled beyond anything I imagined. And Josh going on to help build a little startup called LendingHome, as one of four founding partners. That little company is now called Kiavi—reportedly the largest institutional private lender in America. Worth billions.

Sometimes, a single drop starts a flood.

It's time for you to be that drop—for yourself, and for your family.

Just turn the page and we'll plan your next move.

**For a free copy of my Jerry Maguire epiphany,
The Power Of 6™, just scan the QR code
below and ask for it.**

Conclusion

"Do just once what others say you can't do,
and you will never pay attention to their limitations again."
- Capt. James Cook

Think back to the first page of this book. To the very first thing I asked you.

What would it mean to you if you could add a zero to your income and net worth?

Not just in theory, but for real. A bonafide 10X. What would that actually do for you, for your family…for your ability to have the kind of freedom that truly makes for a happy, meaningful life?

Maybe you've got your answer now. Maybe you're still thinking about it.

But one thing's for sure: in these pages, **you've seen that winning** *The Money Game*—**and adding that extra zero—isn't just possible. It's predictable (I'd argue inevitable)… when you learn to be the bank.**

If you're anything like me, though, you're not just going to sit around and wait around for it to happen.

You want to move faster. Stack wins ASAP.

The solution? Compress time.

Compress Decades Into Days

Everything I know about *The Money Game*—and how to win it—took decades to master.

Let me rephrase that: it took me 85% of my life just to figure it out... and the last 15% to master it.

But you? You have the chance to do exponentially better.

Take my sons, for example. After I *spent* the first 85% of my life learning, they and I *invested* the last 15%—theirs and mine—mastering it together.

Now they're on my level, but 30+ years younger.

That's the real win. They got there *sooner.*

Which means they're not just inheriting wealth fifteen or twenty years from now. They're inheriting wisdom every day. They already have. They helped build it. They own it.

My advice? Do what my sons did. Arbitrage somebody else's time and knowledge. Start from their finish line, inherit their wisdom *now*, and leverage the living crap out of it.

Then, once you've made it yours, model it for others. For your kids, and for theirs.

And please, whatever you do, whoever you do it for—get there *sooner.*

That's the shortcut I want to give you: the ability to pass on wealth and wisdom—to help your family build something bigger, faster, stronger…starting right frickin' now.

Because at the end of the day, a legacy isn't just about what you leave to someone—it's about what you leave in them.

And here's the beautiful part: being the bank is the fastest bridge I know between building wealth and transferring wisdom.

It's our "add a zero" home base. Always will be. Our #1 go-to, day in and day out.

It's seriously the cleanest wealth play I know: Write a check, get a bigger one back, together.

And now it's time to make it *your* wealth play.

This book gave you the roadmap, sure. But roadmaps don't build fortunes. *Action* does.

Ready to start from my finish line? Ready to stop thinking about financial freedom—and start actually building it?

Here's your shortcut: lock in your spot on the waitlist for our *Just Be the Bank* private lending workshop—the only one we offer.

If you're serious about leveling up your skills, compressing decades into days, and dominating *The Money Game* for good, this is your next move.

Don't just watch others create financial freedom. Build yours. Win on your terms. Check it out at www.justbethebank.com.

In that workshop, we hand you the tools. The lending docs. The insider playbook. The real-world strategies to help you implement, scale, and dominate the private lending game—faster than you ever could on your own.

I should know. We didn't have anything like this when we started. We built our business one mistake at a time. If someone had offered to collapse those lessons into a few days, I would've paid a fortune.

Because (and this is huge): *time* is the real currency of your life. Not money. Time.

Why not arbitrage my time instead of spending your own?

Look, we aren't a seminar company. We don't run dozens of programs a year. We have one workshop, *Just Be the Bank: How to Be a Successful Private Lender to Real Estate Flippers.* That's it.

Why only one? Because lending is our superpower. We're arguably the most successful private lending family in America. Who else has done thousands of single-family flipper loans *and* built a fintech lender now reportedly worth billions?

As far as I know, nobody.

"The best arbitrage play in the world is knowledge arbitrage."

And listen: the last thing I want is for you to walk away from this book fired up but frozen. The worst thing you can do is finish these pages, feel inspired…and then do nothing.

If you don't take action, nothing changes. Your money lens stays the same. Your capital remains trapped in mediocre returns. Your financial trajectory never shifts.

Even worse? You set that example for everyone around you.

Think about it: what message are you sending to your kids? To your family? To the people who depend on you? That you found a strategy the wealthy have used for generations—and you chose to leave it on the table?

Right now, there are only two questions you should be asking yourself:

If not for you, WHO? Who are you doing this for? Who in your life needs to see a better way?

If not now, WHEN? When will you finally stop playing their game, and start playing your own?

Join Josh, Blake, and me at www.justbethebank.com—and compress decades into days.

The opportunity is here. The next move—the only move that matters—is yours.

P.S. If you're truly serious about taking control of your financial future, I want to hear from you.

Send me a personal email at **dave@JustBeTheBank.com** and tell me what your biggest takeaway was from this book. I read every email from serious people—because if you're willing to take the time, so am I.

Then, head over to **www.justbethebank.com**, where this journey doesn't end—it begins.

Oh, and one more thing: if you want a free copy of my private lending slide deck—**Just Be The Bank: How You and Your Family Can Create DOUBLE-DIGIT, PASSIVE, RECURRING Income and Wealth**—scan the QR code below or visit www.justbethebank.com/slides.

Let's get to work. Let's add that zero. Together.

And let's build a future so strong, they'll still be talking about it generations from now.

Get the slides to my presentation:
Just Be The Bank: How You and Your Family Can Create DOUBLE-DIGIT, PASSIVE, RECURRING Income and Wealth as a Private Lender

http://www.justbethebank.com/slides

From Red Shield to Rothschild— The Original Private Lender Playbook

The key to your greater future has its roots deep in the past.

And while history likes to glam up this life story, the reality in the early days was pretty hardscrabble and humble.

Maybe that's what lit the fire—a fire that's still burning today, three centuries later, fueled by literally hundreds of billions of dollars. Not through some complex, arcane financial wizardry, but through the same simple strategy I've been showing you throughout this book: being the bank.

Yet before there was that eternal flame, before there was even the hint of a spark, there was a boy.

Twelve years old. Orphaned by smallpox. Shuffled between relatives in an overcrowded apartment just eleven feet across, but home to more than 30 cousins, uncles, and other extended family members—stacked above the family shop in a building marked by a red shield on the door.

In that world, you didn't have the luxury of childhood. If you wanted to eat, you worked. So the boy *worked*.

His money lens, like most of ours in the beginning, was simple: money meant effort.

His family wasn't destitute, but there weren't any silver spoons either. Learning his father's trade wasn't optional. And after a grueling seven-year apprenticeship in a neighboring town, he struck out on his own. It wasn't long before he'd built a robust import-export business and, more importantly, amassed a store of capital.

That's when everything changed.

By the standards of the time, he'd made it. He could've kicked back, lived comfortably, called it good.

But he didn't.

Because when he looked closer—really examined his business—he saw something most people miss: not all parts of his success were created equal. One piece of his operation was pulling more weight than the rest.

The lending.

Moreover, it wasn't physical. It wasn't draining. And it wasn't bound by time. While his trade business required ships, warehouses, and constant motion, lending was clean. Quiet. Scalable. It let him turn a few dollars into more dollars… and more… and more—without grinding himself into the dirt.

Banking back then wasn't what it is today. No skyscrapers. No investment committees. Lending was personal. Local. Relationship-driven. It was private lending in its rawest, most potent form.

And this man, now with capital and clarity, saw the blueprint.

The Family That Mastered the Game

Meyer had five sons. All smart, sharp and well-connected. When they came of age, he placed each of them in a different European capital and set them up as private bankers. They studied the markets. Built networks. Shared intel. And together, they funneled capital into the safest, highest-yielding opportunities on the continent.

One generation in, the family was rich. Two generations in, they were on the shortlist of Europe's most powerful.

And unlike so many who lose it all in a single generation, they didn't flame out. They stuck to their principles. Played the long game.

Today, their descendants still manage banks and oversee assets worth hundreds of billions. The fortune that started in an eleven-foot apartment has become one of the greatest dynasties in financial history.

In time, that orphaned boy built riches so vast, so enduring, that his family name became shorthand for extreme wealth. You know the name, of course. They took it from the red shield mounted above that cramped apartment door: **Rothschild.**

And the real secret behind it all? The same one I've been hammering home in these pages.

The Rothschild legacy—the generational avalanche of wealth—that didn't come from putting money in the bank.

It came from *becoming* the bank.

That was Mayer Rothschild's revelation when he studied his own books: the lending arm quietly outperformed everything. It was the engine—the part of the business that multiplied without friction.

And that engine still runs today.

It's been the cornerstone for our family too, centuries later, in a different world, under vastly different circumstances. And if you've made it this far in the book, I hope it becomes the cornerstone for your family as well.

Like Mayer, you needed your eyes opened. That's what these chapters have been doing.

But now it's time to shift gears. You don't just want insight—you want outcomes. You want to add that extra zero. To turn knowledge into returns.

So let's get moving.

Why You Can—and Should—Build Your Own Family Office

There's a famous case study in generational wealth: the Rockefellers vs. the Vanderbilts.

Both families were once American royalty—titans of the Gilded Age. Both built fortunes so vast they seemed unspendable.

Only one of them still has the money.

Today, the Rockefeller name still conjures billionaire clout. Meanwhile, the most prominent Vanderbilt heir? Anderson Cooper. A household name, sure—but he inherited a mere $1.5 million from his mother, Gloria. That's all that remained of the estate.

So what happened?

The Rockefellers kept control. The Vanderbilts outsourced it.

While the Vanderbilts fumbled their fortune with lavish lifestyles and third-party management, the Rockefellers institutionalized their wealth. They built a family office. They staffed it with family members, not outsiders. They wrote a constitution—literal rules of behavior and investment—to guide every financial decision, across every generation.

They thought like a bank. And they're still reaping the rewards.

Now, here's the kicker: you don't need to be Rockefeller-rich to do this.

We did it. We operate as a family office. You can too.

Not because we had tens of billions, but because we had the right mindset. The right structure. The right playbook.

Our private lending business is run like a *Backpack Family Office*— fully virtual, lean, and scalable from anywhere in the world. It started in a tiny space off Flamingo Road in Vegas. After a couple break-ins, we ditched the office, went remote, and never looked back.

Here's the shift: **Stop thinking of your family *only* as a family. Start thinking of it as a business. A financial entity designed to serve and grow the interests of each member.**

That means keeping the capital in-house. Not trusting it to your broker. Not gambling it on your neighbor's "next big thing." Not getting pulled into your cousin's friend's pre-IPO side hustle.

It means using your family's wealth to build your family's future. Period.

Need legal or tax expertise? Hire it. Everything else? Do it in-house.

The Rockefellers, for instance, lend money *to each other*—not from banks. When a family member needs capital for a house or a business, they make a formal proposal, the family evaluates the deal, and the family earns the interest.

No Wall Street middleman. No luck. Just capital allocation with purpose.

That's how you keep it. That's how you grow it. That's how you create a legacy that lasts.

A Thought Exercise Worth Doing

Take a moment to reflect.

How is your family leveraging its existing wealth and assets for the long-term benefit of everyone involved?

Who actually gets a say in the investments—or the future?

What unspoken rules (or missing frameworks) shape the way your family handles money?

Where are the blind spots—the knowledge gaps that could cost you down the road?

And most importantly… what are you doing to fill them?

In our family, we take a hands-on approach to everything—especially our future. No autopilot. No hoping for the best. That kind of "whatever happens, happens" mindset? It's a straight shot to mediocrity. And if you're holding this book, I'm guessing you're not okay with that either.

Here's what we do instead.

Every October, we come together as a family to reflect—on the last 12 months and the next 12. We each answer 20 questions about what's changed, what matters, and where we're going. From there, we craft our game plan. And while everyone else is coasting through the holidays or scribbling doomed New Year's resolutions, we're already in motion—executing on our next-year plan starting December 1. Together.

We've done this for 14 years straight. And the shift in our lives? Massive.

That simple act—of pausing, planning, and moving with intention—has added zeros to our net worth and stripped stress from our lives. Because here's the truth: my sons and I care more about our future than any outside consultant or portfolio manager ever could. The less of our fate we leave in someone else's hands, the better off we are.

Building Wealth Together—Literally

One of the greatest gifts private lending has given me—beyond control, beyond freedom—is the chance to bring my family into the business. To make money, do good and have fun, every day, with my sons.

But when I worked in corporate, or even in my early entrepreneurial days, that just wasn't possible. There was no room for my sons at the table.

Maybe you've felt that too in your own career. You can't exactly seat an apprentice beside you in your dental practice. You can't drag your kids to court with you. So business becomes a wedge—another thing that pulls you away from the people you love.

Private lending flips that on its head.

You can do deals as a family. You can involve your kids, your spouse, your siblings—or just use the freedom you gain to *be* more present with them. The deals themselves don't take much time. The stress is lower. The returns are higher. And the mood is lighter. It doesn't feel like running a business. It feels like owning your life.

Best of all? You get to shape this thing to fit *your* family. You call the shots. And that kind of control—over your time, your capital, and your legacy—is a force multiplier like no other.

Now, it's time to put these ideas to work.

From our Stech Family heart to yours: we wish you nothing but the best life has to offer. And we hope that somewhere in these pages, something sparked for you—something that helps you add a zero not just to your bank account, but to your life.

Dave, Josh, and Blake
The Stech Family Office

About the Authors

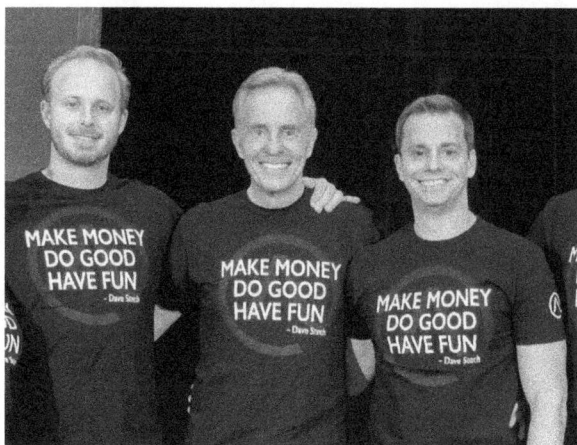

(From left to right: Josh Stech, Dave Stech, Blake Stech)

Dave Stech, Josh Stech, and Blake Stech are real estate and tech angel investors who believe TIMING is the single most important word in investing. And in life.

Beyond their own real estate and tech investments, Dave, Josh, and Blake provide private capital to their network of high-volume house flippers and teach that same "Just Be The Bank" strategy to already successful people who want to add a zero to their incomes and net worth.

Together, in the Stech Family Office, they attracted over $80 million dollars in 2020 for their own operating companies and investment funds in real estate, private lending, and early-stage venture technology. Six billionaires are currently co-investors with them.

Bottom line: The Stech Family Office has cracked the code to make money and not lose it.